Don't Miss It

Four Seasons of Stories
that Spark Enjoyment and Reflection

David Dalke

Printed in the United States of America.

ISBN 978-1-7357323-0-5

Available in paperback, eBook, and audiobook formats at
www.DontMissItStories.com

A Special Thanks

To Sheryl, my dear spouse, whose astute editing eye through many hours of reading and re-reading gently prompted suggestions that spurred me on, so lovingly.

To KC, a cherished member of our family, who guided the birth of this book through his research, wisdom and creativity.

To my ever-loving family, for they are the stories and continue to be very present with their support and encouragement.

To my adventurous friends, especially those who have found themselves on the pages of this book.

To the churches where I served—Pratt, Kansas; Belle Plaine, Kansas; Wichita, Kansas; and Fort Collins, Colorado—who smiled and cried with me as many of these stories unfolded and were shared.

To the worshipping community of the Poudre Canyon chapel, a special place to celebrate the length, breadth and depth of life.

To David Pyle, my friend, who has brought the four seasons to life through his magical artistry.

CONTENTS

INSPIRATION FOR THIS BOOK

As a child I often visited my maternal grandparents. Grandpa and I were magnificent pals. He taught me to spit and say "ain't." Hand in hand, we would walk the three blocks to the ancient town square. We made predictable layovers at Junior's Bakery, Uncle Fred's Drugstore, and the Dime Store. I never returned to the house empty-handed.

Sometimes, I spent hours swaying to-and-fro, and back-and-forth in my Grandpa-created tire swing. With each movement, I imagined flying upward into the fluffy mass of whiteness, shouting orders to the Universe from on high. My pal also built me a treehouse nestled in the thick branches. Securely suspended above the ground, I picked and threw the tree's maturing, green walnuts further than any human being. At Grandpa's, I could be anything I wanted.

At night, we would lay in bed, side by side, and talk about our day. I would say,

"Grandpa, tell me a story."

His creative meanderings were always about rabbits. I listened intently as furry animals chased one another all over town, ate the lettuce in Grandpa's garden, and somehow climbed up the ladder of the water tower to create mischief. Just as the tales would gain momentum, Grandpa would begin to doze off to sleep, his voice dwindling into a rumble like the freight train south of town. I would clear my throat loudly, or accidentally nudge him, and his voice would once again become animated. I loved his stories about himself and those fantastical rabbits.

At an early age, I realized the wonder and redeeming qualities of stories—some made up, some read from a book, and others just shared out of one's own experiences. It is said our brain recalls stories more easily than facts. They are indelibly shaped and scripted in our mind, heart, and soul. Wherever we are, at any given time, there is a story.

I offer my stories to you. They relate to the seasons of our lives. Enjoy them. Reflect on them. See what sparks *insight, illumination—perhaps even an "Aha!"*

SPRING

"Let me tell you a story..."

NOODLES IN MY SOCKS

I never could have dreamed how our lives would become intertwined. He knew me when I was very young—long before I had any awareness of the gigantic impact he would have on the tender minds and hearts of impressionable children. When I was born, he was teaching with my parents in a quaint, Kansas farming community. Waving fields of wheat surrounded the welcoming county seat that announced its name—rather ostentatiously in huge black paint—**ST. JOHN**.

The town square boasted a fountain at the feet of the torch-bearing Lady Liberty. Many ruggedly sandpapered benches greeted the weary who chose not to sit on the soft, green grass. Oft-struggling business owners and well-tanned farmers praying for drops of rain would gather on warm Saturday evenings around seven p.m. to swap stories and check on one another. Once in a while, music would ring out from the welcoming town square, or a dramatic presentation would unfold on a makeshift platform.

My folks taught music in the high school, and Bill taught drama. On many occasions, the three of them would join the Saturday night parade of farmers and town dwellers. Because money was scarce (and teachers' salaries hovered near the lowest pay scale level), Bill lived with my grandparents. Heeding his drive to creatively awaken children's desire for learning, he began to write children's books. Eventually, throughout the next forty years, he spoke to teachers at numerous workshops about the power of rhythm in reading. His name? Bill Martin Jr.

He remained a prolific writer until his death; by that time, he had written over 100 children's books. I remember how Mom would read his first book to me, *A Little Squeegy Bug*. Then came *Brown Bear, Brown Bear, What Do You See?*—which was written in thirty-three minutes on the Long Island railroad train traveling to New York City's Penn Station. These, as well as many other gems, opened up the marvelous world of rhyme and rhythm for precious young minds.

Yes, he knew me and had held me, and now it was time for me to not only hold him in my memory, but to reach out to him and put my arms around him in the twilight of his life. I made a telephone call to one of his publishers in New York City, asking how Bill could be reached. I explained, with quivering voice, how influential he had been in my life as a writer and—more specifically—as a friend of our family. A trusting voice encouraged me.

"Write him a letter and send it to me. I'll see that he gets it."

Ten days later, I received a call from a woman in Texas who asked,

"Is this David?"

"Yes," I replied.

"Bill Martin wants to speak to you."

My heart jumped as my feelings of joy intertwined with disbelief.

I placed my head in one hand, held the telephone closely to my ear with the other, and heard,

"Hello, David? This is Bill Martin. I am so happy to talk to you."

Our visit seemed endless. Now living in his Texas home on Brown Bear Lane, he had an insatiable desire to soak up the events of his missed years in St. John, Kansas. I reminded him of a story told to me throughout the ages of how he and my Dad once threw a football back and forth in my grandparents' living room while I, as a three-year-old, observed the action. There was a resounding crash, then a hole in the picture window, prompting family members to respond with concern and curiosity. I was blamed. The story—frequently repeated, much like an urban legend—continued to be told, and was justified by my uncanny ability to throw with such strength. I asked Bill if he remembered the incident. There was an extended silence, then an obvious change of subject.

We set a time within the next few months, when the weather would be more Spring-like, for a visit to Texas on Brown Bear Lane. As I prepared to hang up, I was at a loss for words as to what the conversation had meant to me. For twenty exciting minutes, we had shared experiences and stories of life and family. This was a childhood hero. I started to say goodbye, only to have him say,

"Oh, David...I was the one who threw the football through the picture window."

And he hung up. If he were to write about that story, it would sound like this: *Bill and Jake looked down with shame, and then with silly smirks on their faces, said little John David was to blame.*

Three months passed and we made our first trip to Brown Bear Lane in Commerce, Texas. Our daughter Julie—now grown, and very familiar with Bill's books—accompanied us on this seemingly once-in-a-lifetime adventure. It was a day filled with conversation, as we shared all that had happened in the years we were out of touch with each other. Bill's dining room table was filled with colorful book layouts that we were privileged to view before they were published—truly a day of unexpected blessings.

Over the next few years, Sheryl and I spent precious times with Bill while sitting in cozy chairs and listening to him tell his life stories, so full of captivating anecdotes. Later in the afternoon, and in need of a change of venue, Bill suggested we go to his favorite restaurant. We carefully helped his increasingly fragile body from his wheelchair and into our car. I'm sure I heard him say, with his eyes twinkling with delight: *Turn here...turn there...the restaurant is in sight.*

Our last trip to Texas was so deeply personal and penetratingly painful. Parkinson's disease was slowly winning the battle of life and death. Bill's tremors were extreme. He shook uncontrollably. Somehow, he remained cheerful amidst the reality of his increasing limitations. This could be our last supper with him, and it felt biblical. That day, he wore his brightly-colored, favorite shirt—a celebration and culmination of years of expression. I said to myself: *It's full of colors you've never seen. There was chicken-chuck-blue, squeegy-bug-yellow and a little bit of froggy-green.*

And with the shirt, he wore his equally colorful, no-nonsense suspenders to hold up his pants.

As Bill sat slightly slumped in his chair, our ever-attentive server briskly approached our table with water in hand.

"Hi, Mr. Martin. So nice to see you!"

Bill politely nodded and glanced up over his eyeglasses. With words that were uttered laboriously, he said,

"These are my good friends. I knew David's parents when he was just a little boy, barely two years old. His parents and I taught together."

She leaned over to Bill, slightly touching his arm as if to acknowledge the struggle of every sentence.

"Can I get you something to drink?"

Bill gestured to his glass of water as if to say,

"This will be sufficient."

He was ready to order, pointing shakily to a pasta dish. Much like an adolescent boy wishing to pretend being grown up and do the impossible, he smiled at us.

It was arduous watching Bill negotiate the slippery noodles from his messy plate to his half-opened mouth. Nothing was easy for him this night, especially with morsels that continued to slip off his silverware like butter off of a hot knife. In a final act of desperation to please his palate, he eyeballed his culinary enemy. Looking down, he began to laugh slightly, then boisterously. Sheryl turned to him and said,

"Bill, something is sure tickling you!"

Without hesitation, a smile stretched across his wrinkled face as he proclaimed,

"I have noodles in my socks!"

Sheryl and I both exclaimed,

"That's the title of your next book!"

Alas, he was not able to write it. A few months later, he left this world, to be seated at the celestial table with his magical mind—and pen in hand.

Assuredly, Bill is continuing to write stories for children, reminding them to love all of life, to listen and to smile—even if you have noodles in your socks.

Thank you, dear friend.

"Let me tell you a story..."

A WELL-KEPT SECRET

There is an old adage: "Some words are better off not said." When does the truth, sometimes scary, serve us or others well and when does it harm ourselves or others? If honesty is the prerequisite to trust or truth, when can lack of honesty be justified to preserve a precious relationship...or to preserve oneself?

I wrestled with the truth of this moment as I felt the pain of her special hole-y paddle on my backside, repeatedly swung at me by the hands of an apologetic elementary school principal.

"David, this hurts me more than it does you!"

Whoever invented such poppycock to justify corporal punishment? Certainly not Mrs. Noel.

I can still picture my fourth-grade classroom. All student seats faced the chalk board. Behind us sat the ever-present shepherd, Mrs. Thresher, with "staff" in hand and eyes constantly surveying her flock—lest any of us would go astray. Beside her desk was a huge metal waste basket. As we would leave the classroom for recess or lunch, it was not unusual to accidentally kick or nudge this symbol of waste control—often on purpose.

My seat was in the row just in front of Mrs. Thresher's perch, four desks from the chalkboard. Behind me sat the most annoying, emotionally grating girl I had ever met in all my ten years. If she wasn't poking her pencil in my back or shoulder, she was carefully whispering something irritating that only increased my desire to shout at her or scream to the universe. Mrs. Thresher handed us a set of questions; she said it wasn't a test. I knew differently. I was sure that my hopes of escaping from her cave of constant mental suffering to another classroom of light and abundance in the fall depended on my answering correctly the aforementioned questions. I began to write, trusting that my pencil had the answers.

In the midst of my mental grappling, there was a hard tap on my shoulder. It came from my nemesis.

"Let me borrow your eraser."

My eraser was a weighty, green, rectangular, hard piece of rubber that could obliterate any of life's mistakes. In utter contempt for her, I flung the missile over my shoulder—missing the object of my consternation. Instead it careened off of the metal waste basket—scaring the wits out of Mrs. Thresher—and causing all of my classmates to be temporarily airborne.

As the bell rang signaling time for lunch, I felt saved. I handed in my paper and moved gingerly towards the door, only to hear a firm and punitive voice say,

"David, please sit down!"

A further command flew my way.

"Come with me. We are going to Mrs. Noel's office."

In my thinking, I was about to experience a misuse of power that was reinforced by the word "Principal" printed across her thick, wooden door. Sure enough, the conversation was a one-way street, with Mrs. Thresher telling her side of the story. No one allowed me to plead my innocence and justifiable frustration with my annoying classmate. The command was given,

"Bend over."

Three rather firm strokes were delivered. I left the chamber of punishment, running quickly home for a belated lunch break. With each step of the way I plotted how to give my Mom a rational reason for my being fifteen minutes later than usual. This beautiful spring day could become ugly. When questioned, I simply said with false pride, definitely not looking up from my sandwich,

"I stayed to visit with my teacher about something I didn't understand."

The rule at our home was this: if you receive a spanking at school, you will also receive one at home—no questions asked. For years, I carried in my guilty conscience the picture of that wooden paddle. I also grappled with the question: *When does the scary truth serve us well and when does it harm us?* I knew the answer.

I was home from college celebrating my 21st birthday. Presents were unwrapped, hugs of gratefulness were given in return, and then came the moment for my long-awaited confession. I looked at my parents and spoke apologetically:

When I was in the fourth grade—you know, Mrs. Thresher's class? Well, Mom, you probably don't remember my coming home late for lunch one day, but the reason I was late, um, I got a spanking for something I did, and I knew if I told you and Dad I would get another spanking at home, so I waited until now to tell you.

Everyone smiled, fully understanding my delay.

My decision in waiting eleven years to disclose the truth of my absolutely worst day in fourth grade was safe strategy and truly an act of wisdom. I still remember—with disdain—that annoying creature who sat behind me in Mrs. Thresher's class—and who "gave this story legs."

SACKED AT THE GROCERY STORE

Saturdays are days to "do today what you said yesterday that you would do tomorrow." I slowly and thoughtfully open my closet door. Staring at me are thick-soled, unpolished boots, a pair of permanently stained Levi's, and a flannel shirt with missing buttons, torn at the elbows and frayed at the cuffs. Dressed and mildly eager for the tasks before me, I am ready to challenge the day of reckoning before the apocalypse is upon us.

This day, it is the garage that beckons for my attention. It is time for spring cleaning. Waiting there for me is an eclectic array of household items, dusty used books, greasy gas cans, snow shovels and rarely-used tools. A slight, cool breeze from the open garage door complicates my well-intentioned task, as plastic sacks—seemingly hundreds of them—begin artistically blowing about the garage, playing a game of "catch me if you can." I corral them one at a time and stuff them into six large bags. Heading to a place that is environmentally aware is now the priority. The rest of the garage can wait.

Do you see Saturdays as a gift like I do? The best part is not shaving or showering. On this particular day I gladly look unbelievably scruffy with no fears of judgment. My spouse,

Sheryl, an ecological advocate, directs me to a neighborhood grocery store.

"David, they accept recycling of plastic bags."

I loaded them in the car and set off to do my part in protecting and preserving our planet.

The huge parking lot—which also provides spaces for a popular pizza establishment, a massage franchise, New York style delicatessen, and a family restaurant—is frustratingly full. I slowly drive around, following several vehicles all waiting to snag the first empty space. Then it happens. In the farthest reaches of the parking facility a wide-open spot appears. It isn't my preferred choice. I want to be near the front of the grocery store entrance, knowing I must make several treks with my recycling bags. I open my car door, take a deep breath, eye the distance to the welcome sign well over one hundred yards away, and turn to grab my first load.

Out of nowhere, behind my crammed-full car and near a fence, looms a grocery cart. It's not just any grocery cart. It is like an eighteen-wheeled, motor-less transporter. I push it gingerly towards the car. Carefully, I open the back door and begin loading one bag after another. I continue to load the cart. Lo and behold (as my Daddy used to exclaim), I am now ready to enter the store and I can do it in one trip! I proceed, dodging cars looking for spaces and pedestrians looking for lost cars.

I walk through the automatic doors, gazing about for the recycling bins. A young worker, obviously employed at the non-executive level, spots me and quickly turns away. Maybe scruffy is too nice a word to describe my tousled hair, unshaven face and my Saturday attire. Eagerly I said,

"Excuse me...I have all these plastics and want to know where to take them."

I wasn't asking him to escort me, just to point the way. Instead, he gives me a judgmental head-to-toe scanning, points toward my huge cart of recycling materials, and waves to another employee who is carrying out her responsibilities as a checkout clerk. She peers around her customer who is fumbling for his credit card. Soon the transaction is completed, and the two employees continue their silent communication with one another.

Pressing her lips together, she shakes her head from left to right several times. It is a universal communication that silently shouts "NO!" The nervous young man, standing next to me and shifting from one leg to the other, says,

"Um...well, we don't do recycle."

After experiencing dismissal from these two employees, my now-edgy voice conveys my intensity. I say,

"Well, my wife told me you have a place in this store where I could leave these plastic bags."

It was obvious I was being rejected. He repeated, almost mumbling, and looking down,

"We don't recycle."

I wheel my chock-full grocery basket to the other side of the store, dodging oncoming customers who are entering checkout lines. Nearing the produce counters, I notice another young man who is placing lettuce and cabbage on a water-drenched and dripping shelf. He turns and greets me with a smile. I say,

"Excuse me, but I understand you have a place in the store for recycling."

Without hesitation, he gladly says,

"We sure do. It's in the back. Here, let me take your cart. I'll handle it."

I am grateful and incensed at the same time! I have a new awareness of what it means to "walk in another person's shoes." I have come to this store to do my environmental duty and am treated like an undesirable. I debate how to handle my feelings. *Do I talk to a manager? Do I go back to the young employee I first encountered and educate him? What about the head-shaking woman at the cash register?* I grab a loaf of bread and head to her checkout line. As I place my one item on the conveyer belt, she looks sheepishly at me. I say firmly,

"You know, you DO have a place to recycle in this store!"

Embarrassed, she says in a low voice,

"I really thought you wanted money for all those bags."

As she handed me my change, I said,

"I look this way because I'm cleaning out my garage."

I turned and walked out.

The sun rises and the sun sets. That we can count on. The mystery is what happens to us when we unknowingly find ourselves in another person's shoes.

HUNGRY FOR GOOD NEWS

Today is Saint Patrick's Day, March 17th, and I am remembering an experience from 1961. While we rushed to catch a plane for my Grandma's funeral in Kansas, my brother-in-law and I created a shortcut and side-stepped our way through the huge St. Paddy's Day parade in New York City. As I was reminiscing, right in the midst of my musings, my spouse suggested that I join her upstairs in our small office to begin filling out some paperwork we had been avoiding. I would have much rather continued relaxing and remembering the excitement of the parade. It was 6:00 o'clock in the evening.

As we worked together, a sound penetrated our thoughts. It was an eerie, rather high-pitched vibration that cut through television noise and the tapping of the computer keys. I asked,

"Sheryl, do you hear that sound?"

She paused. We both wondered if it came from our TV downstairs. I peered over the edge of the loft, hearing only pandemic news. I went downstairs and scanned the back yard—nothing. I glanced out our front door that overlooked the grassy courtyard, which was surrounded by five other homes whose front doors also faced into the common area. All of a sudden, the sound made perfect sense.

On this holiday our next-door neighbor had invited her boyfriend to play his bagpipe in the front yard for her neighbors. He was clad in the traditional Scottish attire, and played the pipes' unique melody notes along with its sustained drones for a few of us in this concerned and questioning world. For weeks, our neighborhood had been abnormally quiet, with most of us staying indoors to protect ourselves from the virus.

As I stood in awe of the music pouring forth from this young piper, I noticed front doors opening and neighbors emerging—all keeping their distance. Some brought chairs; others chose to just stand in silence to hear the music. One neighbor shuffled slowly along the sidewalk to get closer. We all smiled and waved at one another when we caught each other's eye. We were a community.

With an explanation of each piece of music, he played one number after another as the sun began to ease toward the horizon. In unison we applauded. The moment was so special for us all, hungering for good news during this worrisome time. I was reminded of the folks in Europe clapping nightly for all their coronavirus first responders, and singing solos of hope from their open windows. I thought of the two young cellists on their front porch in Ohio, playing for their elderly neighbor. And then there were the three people in New Hampshire playing various instruments, waking their neighbors to a more hopeful new day.

Our piper proceeded to play his last number—"Amazing Grace":

AMAZING GRACE, HOW SWEET THE SOUND
THAT SAVED A SOUL LIKE ME.
I ONCE WAS LOST, BUT NOW AM FOUND,
WAS BLIND, BUT NOW I SEE.

We all stood in silence as we continued to relish the gift of music. His playing was a well-timed entry into our lives that only a few minutes before had been so isolated.

MORE THAN THE EXTRA MILE

Our family loves to be together. In some ways, that is a strange statement since we are all scattered miles apart. But, we make it happen. And this particular time was no different—full of laughter, good food, old stories and the anticipation of new experiences.

We were in South Carolina visiting our oldest grandson and his wonderful, caring wife. While driving through the lush countryside, I noticed a sign overlooking the road that read, "Spartanburg Methodist College." I immediately remembered a story about this college, that surely made a lasting impact on the life of several athletes, their coaches, and the President of this small church-related institution.

Ah, but there is another school in the Midwest that first needs our attention.

As long as I can remember, Hutchinson Junior College, nestled unobtrusively in the middle of Kansas, hosts the National Junior College basketball tournament. Besides the state fair, this event is the most anticipated happening in the lives of the 40,000 hard-working townsfolk. Farmers leave their tractors, some businesses in the area modify their hours, and families drive long distances with their packed lunches to spend their days at the arena watching one game after another. The exciting week ushers in Spring, with new blossoms and loud shouts in an historic gymnasium. Many sport aficionados say that, year after year, it is some of the most outstanding basketball one could ever imagine.

So, where does Spartanburg Methodist College fit into this picture? Out of the benevolent spirit of the National Junior College Athletic Association, this small, two-year school of 800 students, was invited to compete in the national basketball tournament. It was truly a gift and a welcomed overture. It was also 1,320 miles from this quaint campus in South Carolina to the middle of the wheat state. With no money to fly, the team and two coaches boarded a bus for the journey. Rumbling down the road mile after mile, going to an unfamiliar destination where there would be no one in the stands to shout encouragement, the busload of grateful and anxious athletes pressed on.

Prior to their leaving, the President of this little-known Methodist school decided to test what it means to practice what we preach. If clergy were claiming from their pulpits that we must be caring and loving to one another, then now is the time to put our feet to the fire. The President wrote to the District Superintendent of the United Methodist Church in the Hutchinson area. She simply asked,

"Would you be willing to publicize our games to your various church congregations and encourage those interested in attending to cheer for us? I know our young team would appreciate a cheering section."

She signed her name, then added,

"Thank you for considering what must seem like a 'wacked-out' request."

It had been a very long trek through several states. Questions had been bantered about from one anxious athlete to another.

"Are we good enough to be here?"

"What will it be like to not have any of our fans rooting for us?"

The bus slowly pulled in front of the downtown hotel. As one of the coaches exited to begin verifying sleeping arrangements with the staff, he was greeted by a large group of folks—holding up welcoming signs—eager to offer ample amounts of snack food and sports drinks to each athlete. Waiting for their room assignments, the players lounged in the lobby, reading special cards from children, each one carefully made in their Sunday School classes. The President's "wacked-out" request had been given careful and joyful attention by several churches in the area.

After the team's first practice, they were surrounded by members of another congregation who brought them homemade cookies. The momentum of going the extra mile continued with many folks from two other local churches committing themselves to attending their first game. All wore white t-shirts featuring the Spartanburg Methodist College logo. The shirts had been sent overnight by the school's President. Seventy-five eager fans of all ages continuously shouted words of encouragement, with a few semi-organized cheers. Spartanburg Methodist College won their game. At its conclusion, the players turned to applaud their newly-adopted fan club, still lingering in the stands. It was a tender moment.

After the tournament had concluded and the team had returned to their familiar surroundings, the President of the College offered the following heartfelt words:

I have been employed in the United Methodist connectional system for fifteen years at two different institutions. However, I have never experienced what it means to connect with one another like those few days in Hutchinson, Kansas.

It was more than going the extra mile.

"Let me tell you a story..."

A Song For Nellie

She was older than the rest of us by some forty years. Her uncombed, silver-streaked hair complimented the plain, out-of-style dress she wore every day. She could have easily been described as "frumpy." Her hands appeared rough, obviously in need of some soothing lotion to nurture the visible cracks in her skin. She carried a large, well-worn, fake leather purse, which served as storage for personal items and an abundance of books. Her name was Nellie. She was classified as a non-traditional student in this small Quaker college. She had a thirst for learning. Nellie was my classmate.

In the three years that we shared noisy hallways, required chapel services, often-stimulating classes and unhealthy cafeteria snacks, I don't recall hearing her speak a word. Her steadfast silence was as noticeable as the many raised hands in classes. B.B. King, the accomplished guitarist, said,

"The beautiful thing about learning is nobody can take it away from you."

Indeed, Nellie was a learner. I wanted to know more about her.

I grew up in a very musical family. Some of my fondest memories were listening to my Mom and Dad sing duets at our annual family reunion in little ol' Goessel, Kansas. In a pitted cement-floored church basement they would lovingly look at one another as their voices blessed the appreciative relatives with their rendition of "My Hero." A 19th century German philosopher, Friedrich Nietzsche, said,

"Without music, life would be a mistake."

My sister and I heard that prophetic message. We were born to carry on our family's musical legacy.

I never fancied myself a soloist. Neither did my choir director in college. In fact, Dr. Mayer suggested I take voice lessons—so I would not be so *outstanding* in the second tenor section. However, I did fit in—and blended splendidly—with three buddies who had melodious voices. We became a quartet. While Nellie was quietly absorbing knowledge, we were causing the leaves to quiver with our rendition of "Coney Island Baby". A few close-harmony hymns dotted our repertoire, as well.

During my senior year, our quartet was asked to sing at the annual school awards banquet, held each spring. Professors, high-achieving students, and many supportive non-recipients were present. Four rows back in the auditorium, nestled alone, was Nellie.

We warbled several lively numbers—with humorous gestures and facial expressions. One last song remained. We had worked up a number entitled "Seeing Nellie Home". It was a ballad—with moments of upbeat harmonies. Noticing our friend in the fourth row, vacant seats beside her, we compassionately decided in advance to not only dedicate our last number to her, but look directly into her pleasant face as we sang. Gesturing towards Nellie, Carl announced our intentions. His simple and genuine words matched her quiet demeanor. Looking tenderly at her, we began:

IN THE SKY THE BRIGHT STARS GLITTERED.
ON THE BANK THE PALE MOON SHONE.
IT WAS FROM AUNT DINAH'S QUILTING PARTY,
I WAS SEEING NELLIE HOME.

ON MY ARM A SOFT HAND RESTED,
RESTED LIGHT AS OCEAN FOAM.
IT WAS FROM AUNT DINAH'S QUILTING PARTY,
I WAS SEEING NELLIE HOME.

ON MY LIFE NEW HOPES WERE DAWNING,
AND THOSE HOPES HAVE LIVED AND GROWN.
IT WAS FROM AUNT DINAH'S QUILTING PARTY,
I WAS SEEING NELLIE HOME.

Hans Christian Andersen, the Danish short story writer, eloquently said,

"Where words fail, music speaks."

For the first time in three years, Nellie spoke to us—with tears of joy—that cascaded down her beautifully-aged cheeks.

"Let me tell you a story..."

LIFE LESSONS FROM A BOOKCASE

Someone whispered in my ear,

"This is your last semester in college. Take a class you know nothing about."

Maybe it was my Grandpa, who toiled every day in the tiny, confined space of his tool shed. It could have been my Dad, who knew I had no knowledge or experience of how to craft the simplest of bookends from a spiritless piece of wood into a monument on the mantle. I enrolled in Woodworking 101.

Life is about making plans. Often the goal is clear. Other times it is uncertain. Either way, the pencil in our mind begins to sketch the next steps. Sitting at a well-worn, wooden bench, I began to compose the dimensions for my bookcase, which would be carved and refined out of birds-eye maple. Different colored drawing pencils created certain dimensions for the three shelves. I labored intensely between simplicity and flamboyance in the desired outcome. Several pieces of crumpled potential plans cluttered the floor around my work bench. I needed to give my non-calloused hands their best chance to succeed in this project.

Two weeks into the semester, Professor Hubert Wiebe approached my workspace. He was highly skilled in arts and crafts. His gentle and caring Mennonite background created a non-judgmental atmosphere as he spoke to me.

"David, what are you doing?"

I felt confident in my answer. With great pride I said,

"Professor Wiebe, I am making the plans for my bookcase!"

He looked at my drawings. Taking a deep breath, he invited me to stand up by my bench and look around the busy, noisy room full of my classmates, all diligently and industriously working on their projects. He said,

"What do you see?"

I replied, "Well, there's Gerald sanding his chair. And Lois working on her lamp. Lawrence is putting the finishing touches on his table...and..."

He interrupted me and thoughtfully asked once again,

"So David, what are you doing?"

Emphatically, I repeated my answer. "I am making the plans for my bookcase."

He nodded and moved on.

In retrospect, I thought of the anxiety I felt when our mentor invited all of us to "Go draw your wood." That was a foreign language.

There were moments when Professor Wiebe stepped out of the room, and then I would entice fellow students to cut my measured and marked shelves on the band saw, so I wouldn't risk losing a digit...or two. However, after bribing Keith to cut my wood for me, I fearfully stood near the whirling machine. As he proceeded, a piece of wood kicked back from the saw, hitting my little finger which was hanging out of the pocket of my jeans. Pain! Fearing to look down at my throbbing little finger, I said to myself, *I think it's gone!*

The piece of wood further careened across the room, striking a "fellow carpenter" in the back.

"Ouch! What was THAT?" he yelled.

My good buddy, John, took me to the emergency room for a repair of my broken finger. Upon my return to campus many fellow woodworkers had added finishing touches to my bookcase, which apparently had become a class project.

Today, that class project sits upstairs in our home, full of reading material and memorabilia. I look at it often, with fond memories of that last semester in a room full of dust, wood-shavings and the lingering smell of shellac. That day, while I continued to draw my plans and my classmates were busily at work on their projects, I learned a life lesson. My simple, hoped-for masterpiece would not exist if it had not been for one question from my caring instructor. Professor Wiebe simply asked,

"So, David, when are you ever going to build your bookcase?"

Beverly Sills, the beautiful voice of the Metropolitan Opera, said,

"You may be disappointed if you fail, but you are doomed if you don't try."

"Let me tell you a story..."

SLIDING DOWN THE WALL

My mom told this story over and over. Each time, her animated expressions resonated like a small child opening presents on Christmas Eve. She was the self-appointed chaperone in my dad's high school band. She, along with other parents, drove budding musicians to their state band festivals, district contests, and national marching, concert and sight-reading extravaganzas, which were often hosted on university campuses. Her recounting of those pilgrimages was flooded with anecdotes, which she relished sharing.

One story rose above the rest.

"Do you remember when..." she would repetitiously begin:

...the band was playing in the district contest in Dodge City? If they took first place, they would go to Colorado Springs to the nationals in May, only one month away. It was lots of pressure on the kids. They had practiced so hard and wanted to win so badly. Jake had selected a very challenging number for their finale. I'm sure you remember Donny Shepherd. Well, he was a fine brass player, and this number had a very difficult baritone solo in it. It started very low, and then climbs slowly to an extremely high pitch. In practices he often could not hit that last note. It was so hard for him. My hands were wringing wet every time he began his solo.

I beamed inside as I witnessed her zest to invite us on this storytelling journey. She continued:

The band played with such precision and blended tones that day. Then came the last number. I'm still not sure why Jake selected it, but I just trusted his judgment—poor Donny!

Taking a deep breath and gesturing with her hands, mom stumbled for more words:

I spotted Donny through the French horn and trombone sections. I...um, just wanted to nod at him with a warm smile. Jake waved his baton in a downward motion. The band stopped. There was a brief moment of silence. Donny began. I knew the first part of his solo was the easiest. His sounds filled the auditorium. As he began to climb up the scale towards that high note, I could feel my body rising from my chair in unison with him.

Mom would always pause her story, leaving the listeners wanting more:

I had a silent visit with God, not knowing if it made any difference...but I did ask for Donny to hit that note. That's all—just hit the note! Someone heard my words because Donny played that note like the angels blowing their celestial trumpets. He held the unbroken sound for at least three seconds.

Reliving this captivating memory, she continued:

I went backstage after the band finished. I hugged so many of the kids, all of them sensing they had played well enough to go to the national contest. There was Donny, leaning against the wall, with sweat dripping down his cheeks. He had loosened his tie and unbuttoned his woolen band jacket. As I approached him, he smiled so big at me. "Hi, Mrs. Dalke." I looked at him and said, "Oh Donny, you played the best you have ever played." Then he said, "Well, I knew if I didn't hit that note—God would, and sure enough God did!"

And he slid down the wall in a dead faint.

The story always warmed my soul. Don't know if there was any theological significance wrapped around this frequently-repeated tale, but whenever I have needed bolstering in my life's wonderings, I think of Mom, Dad's band, and a young man named Donny—who hit the unreachable.

"Let me tell you a story..."

HE PUT HIS PENCIL DOWN

Going to Drew Theological Seminary in Madison, New Jersey, 1500 miles from home, was the best decision of my then-twenty-two years of life. Even though I was apprehensive, I still wanted more education. It is a school twenty-five miles from New York City, and known for having the finest faculty of any Methodist seminary in the United States. I thought to myself...*you have to be kidding me, is this real?*...but here I was with my Dad helping to pack the car for an adventure yet to unfold.

My senior pastor, Dr. Ron Meredith, had guided me throughout my restless years of high school and college. We visited many times. His demeanor and caring for me created a special bond. Then came a life-altering question amidst his many nuggets of wisdom:

> David, why don't you consider going to Drew? I loved it. Their faculty ranks at the top, including my classmate, Carl Michalson who is plowing one furrow after another planting seeds of spiritual inquiry and growth. He—and he alone—would be worth your three years of study.

So, I applied to Drew Theological Seminary. My hand shook with trepidation as I put my application in the mail. Why would this school—nestled in the lush New Jersey forest, with a huge statue of Francis Asbury sitting upon a beautifully-sculpted horse—want me?

Ten days later, an envelope appeared in our mailbox. Not only had I been accepted to Drew, I was also offered a scholarship to teach swimming at the local YMCA. I remember my stomach doing flip-flops with disbelief, feeling gratefulness to Dr. Meredith for his guidance, and a renewal of my own fear of intellectual inadequacy. I wondered if Friends University had prepared me for my journey into the theological world of Barth, Brunner, Niebuhr and Tillich. Then, I remembered the reassuring words from my mentor:

"Lean on my friend Carl Michalson. He will stand by you."

I enrolled in every class I could that Dr. Michalson taught. Whether sitting in his downstairs office in Seminary Hall— just the two of us—where his gentle spirit was always so welcoming, or hanging on his every word in class, he was stimulating and thought-provoking, reaffirming my decision to attend this school.

It was in my final year, in the last-semester class seminar, when he helped me understand how our logical left brain and our right brain of feelings blended into one another. The seminar was on prayer, with only twelve of us enrolled. It felt like a tutorial and I was sitting at the feet of the master. Dr. Michalson had that kind of subtle effect on each of us as we experienced the dynamics of prayer, silent or spoken.

At the beginning of each three-hour class, he would ask one of us to pray. From our training, we would assume the traditional position of head bowed, eyes closed, and for some of us, hands clasped—except for Dr. Michalson, who would make notes about the prayer and give feedback to the "pray-er" after the emphatic "Amen."

On this particular afternoon, Dr. Michalson asked Paul to pray. I didn't know Paul very well, but found him to be a soft-spoken, gangly-looking, aspiring theologian who blended into the background. He began to pray. In past weeks, some of the opening prayers had seemed rather perfunctory, often reminding me of a rambling car without a road map. At the long table we sat, much like ancient knights in the King's Court. I could hear the pencil scribbling thoughts while Paul prayed.

His words were spoken with tender, unrehearsed eloquence. The room grew quieter. It started to feel like a haven of hope into which all of us had been drawn. We were enveloped in silence, except for the quiet, barely-audible words from Paul. Overcome by the spirit of the prayer, Dr. Michalson embraced the moment.

Paul spoke his last plea for guidance with gratefulness to God, and we all sat quietly in meditation for several minutes. Then Dr. Michalson spoke compassionately.

"Paul, I started to critique your prayer, like every other class session. But I couldn't make my pencil write. I found myself praying your prayer with you. I had to lay my pencil down. I couldn't critique your prayer, only experience it."

Some of life's happenings stay locked in our memories forever. For me, this was one of them. What happened that day on the second floor of that old seminary building was so unexpected. We became immersed in something holy. And at the head of the table sat a professor who allowed himself to humbly BE in the moment as he put his pencil down.

SUMMER

"Let me tell you a story..."

DANCING AT THE POWWOW

"Welcome to Mother Earth," said the Lakota Elder.

His name was Peter.

You have come to the place where the suicide rate is the highest in the United States. You have come to an area where poverty is the worst. You have also come to a place where longevity for people that live here is forty-four years for a man and forty-seven years for a woman. Here we get up at three o'clock in the morning and drive forty-eight miles to go shop at a Walmart so people won't stare at us who are from the reservation.

He continued:

Thank you for fixing up our roofs and building our ramps, so people won't have to take wheelchairs down steps. Thank you for washing many jars so we are able to do canning. Thank you for painting and reconditioning our homes. Thank you for playing with the children at the Boys and Girls Club.

He was speaking so fervently to our church youth groups from South Carolina and Colorado. We united our energies for one week at the Crow Creek Reservation in South Dakota. The winds of learning and cultivating relationships swept over youth and sponsors. Values had been challenged. Responsibility for history was no longer taken for granted. A deepened appreciation for our own circumstances back home was gratefully recounted.

As the summer sun rose on our last work day, our Lakota friend issued an invitation.

"Come to the PowWow. It will be tonight at seven o'clock. Come to the PowWow."

All of us attended. We observed the elders and children and people of all ages dancing to the rhythmic low sound of the drum. Abruptly, the dancing stopped. Peter, our Lakota companion, called all of us to the middle of the field. He addressed everyone at the PowWow.

"I want to let you all know we have two groups here from Colorado and South Carolina. I want to thank them because they're beautiful people."

He said it again.

"They are beautiful people. I want to invite them to dance with us."

We joined our Native American friends one step at a time. All of a sudden someone looped my arm in theirs. It was my daughter Julie, one of the sponsors from the South Carolina youth group. We danced joyfully together. And then, someone took my other arm. It was Elizabeth, my granddaughter. Three generations dancing together and introspectively asking the same questions:

How did we get here? and *Can we make a difference now?*

In that moment I realized I cannot change history, the Trail of Tears or Wounded Knee. With values shaken and stirring inside of us, we danced on, the three of us together, with our Lakota friends. What is left to say or do? Keep loving. Keep asking to be forgiven. Keep dancing.

HOSES AND COOKIES

Church ministry can require multiple hats. I wore many of them. In addition to consulting in local churches I also developed a pastoral counseling practice. I would see healthy folks who just wanted to be healthier. Except for Roy. His mom—with tears and a look of hopeful expectation—asked me to work with Roy.

"He remembers you. I took him to church one time when you were a guest preacher and he whispered to me, 'Mommy, I like him.' Please, maybe just a few times? He has so many problems and the biggest is loving himself."

I said,

"Sure, I'll see him. How about this week sometime?"

Often, we need to follow our intuition—that voice inside our heart and soul that seems to nudge us one direction or another. In that moment of intuitive awareness we make a decision as to how we will use our energy. Roy was twenty-two years old when he entered my life—and had the mind of an eight-year-old. He was locked into that childlike state of being simple and free of blame, in a world that was not always prepared to welcome him.

The day for his appointment came. I did not expect to learn the many lessons about life that I would from this little boy in a big boy's body. Surprisingly, he drove himself to my office. I watched from the window as he carefully closed the door to an old, battered pickup truck. Roy was slim in stature with tanned arms from mowing the neighbor's lawns. He slowly walked up the sidewalk, face hidden under a dirty, beat-up Denver Broncos ballcap, to tap lightly on the door.

He sprawled out on the couch, sipping a glass of cold water. Roy told me he was working three days a week at a nursery watering trees and plants. Inwardly, I felt grateful he had been given a job nurturing God's beauty. He was obviously feeling a huge sense of accomplishment as only an eight-year-old would.

The next week our time together felt more like we had meshed. We took a walk and talked, stopping by the Dairy Queen for a fast-melting ice cream cone. Throughout the months we met, my admiration for this innocent young man grew. I often felt that his words of wisdom fed my soul and I was full of gratitude for his coming into my life.

On one of our walks we stumbled along a railroad track that seemed to narrow into infinity. Roy stopped and looked at me.

"My Daddy died."

I said, "Yes, I know. I'm sure that makes you very sad, and I'm sorry."

He continued.

"He was an engineer on a train."

Roy rarely talked about his Dad, and only minimally, mentioning that he missed him. Walking the tracks stimulated another memory. Balancing his hands on the rocky ground, he leaned down and carefully put his ear to the rail. Looking up at me, with hope in his voice, he said,

"There's a train coming. Maybe it's my Daddy."

Every time we met, the Dairy Queen beckoned us. I believe Roy would walk miles for an ice cream cone. Our time together was almost over. As we neared his unwashed truck he fumbled for his keys. Roy looked up at me, almost as if he had waited until the end of our visit to muster up the courage to tell me,

"Tomorrow will be my last day working at the nursery. They told me not to come back."

My first impulse was to run as fast as I could to that workplace, to tell them what an injustice they had imposed on this beautiful young man who simply believed in doing the right thing in this mixed-up world. However, I have learned it is best to avoid acting on my first impulse, so I just listened to his thoughts about tomorrow—his last day of work.

"When I go to work tomorrow, do you know what I'm going to do?"

I remained silent with no expectation as to what I would hear.

"I'm going to bake them all some cookies. And then, do you know what else I'm going to do?"

I thought, *finally, here is where his anger is going to come out, and he'll be able to express how unfair it feels to be let go from a job that means so much to him.* He said,

"Tomorrow, before I leave, I'm going to roll up the hoses the very best they have ever been rolled up!"

I miss him and all that he taught me.

LOVE AFFAIR WITH THE CIRCUS

Recently I read the newspaper headline with sadness. "Ringling Brothers Barnum and Bailey Circus Gives Final Show to Sellout Crowd." The ever-present time machine in my head swept me back into an energetic fifth grader who fell in love once a year with the most famous circus in the world.

It was a hot, humid, wind-blown day, where loud blasts from a weather-beaten engine announced the arrival of a child's dream. Creating a rumbling noise on the rails south of town, the train screeched to a halt. Doors opened and ramps lowered with a bang from the elevated box cars. Caged animals and their brave handlers descended to the hot pavement, everyone lumbering slowly toward the fairgrounds.

The circus was an annual summer affair that caused a child's stomach to flip-flop and a parent's heart to beat with joy, knowing the weekend could be spent under the huge canvas tent. Memories of cotton candy; oohs and aahs while staring upwards at the high-wire; twenty brightly-colored clowns exiting one by one from the tiniest of vehicles; scantily-clad daredevils standing on the backs of tandem galloping horses; Clyde Beatty wannabees cracking their whips at growling tigers and lions so regally perched on their stools; elephants propping their gigantic legs on one another to form a horizontal line of grey, thick skin, and the booming voice of the ring-master bellowing,

"Welcome to The Greatest Show On Earth!"
It was sensory overload...how easy to remember.

The next morning, Saturday, I rode my Schwinn bicycle faster than a speeding bullet toward the fairgrounds. Playing cards, strategically placed in the spokes, created a loud sound that broadcasted my single-minded intensity for speed. I just knew there was a place for me with this circus. They needed me. I even wondered what it would be like to travel with them from town to town. Of course, I did not discuss such a far-fetched fantasy with Mom or Dad. I pedaled faster. The afternoon show would begin in two hours.

As I approached the busy fairgrounds, skidding my bike tires in my signature abrupt stop, a friendly circus employee gestured to me. He was clad in dirty old jeans, but had a wondrous windbreaker that read, "The Greatest Show On Earth." I wanted a jacket just like that one! I watched him water the elephants while all the time listening to the noisy preparation nearby in the huge tent, for the afternoon show. I was in awe. The man spoke:

"Want to work for the circus? They're setting up now. I think they need help with the chairs, so do some work now and I'll give you a free pass for the afternoon performance tomorrow."

Turning back to the elephants, he said,
"Come around 11:00. I'll have your ticket."

I hustled to the tent to assist in chair-setting. The circus band was rehearsing while performers warmed up and walked around the arena becoming familiar with the new setting. Every show was unique. The eager crowd began to come early as I set the last chair near the entrance. Here the well-trained animals and courageous performers would come forth, with hands waving, blowing kisses and striking impossible poses. I wanted to stay, but the man had said to come tomorrow and he would give me my free ticket.

My heart beat faster than my legs were pedaling as I approached my house. I waited until supper to tell Mom and Dad about my visit with the nice man watering the huge elephants and his promise to me of a ticket for tomorrow, a Sunday performance. Trepidation was in my voice as I sought their permission to miss Sunday School and Church, but the negotiation went in my favor and they lovingly supported my adventure. Needless to say, I barely slept that night. Whether awake or asleep, the circus occupied my total being. I had earned my way and my reward was in sight.

As I approached the usually hectic fairgrounds my whole being felt lost. There were no tents. No cages. No one was wandering around with balloons in hand shouting, "Welcome To The Greatest Show On Earth!"

Only a faint odor of the magnificent animals remained. The circus was gone. They must have packed up in the middle of the night after their late show. The loaded circus train had chugged off to the next town.

I will never let that memory of sounds, smells, excitement and a friendly circus handyman's promise escape me. Maybe he just forgot that the circus was leaving in the middle of the night, and there would be no tomorrow. Regardless, I learned at an early age that what is often said may not always be the truth. I also learned as I got older, that there are some truths in this ol' world that are worthy of holding onto. As the ring master would always say as the lights dimmed and applause waned,

"We'll see you down the road!"

"Let me tell you a story..."

THROW STRIKES

Summer and fun activities are synonymous with swimming in the neighborhood pool, going to movies in the middle of the day, planning vacations, and baseball—known as America's pastime—or, more accurately for some households, an all-consuming two-month obsession. As classroom teachers say "goodbye," softball and baseball coaches say "hello." The umpire's voice, shouting out the familiar "Batter UP!" welcomes the season that dictates a family's summer schedule.

Two of our grandchildren have been Rebels since they were six years old. To clarify, they played on the Rebels baseball team for eight years. Balls, bats, mitts, uniforms, water bottles and snacks were the staples that filled the trunk of the family car throughout summer months. Friday through Sunday they would load up and travel to neighboring states for weekend games and tournaments.

Often between games or in evenings, coaches and parents would plan activities that highlighted local attractions. Together the team would visit historical landmarks, amusement parks, famous restaurants or go swimming. This trip was no different.

One particular year we decided to join the Rebel community for their tournament to watch our grandson play. The eleven-hour drive to Oklahoma City was worth the anticipation. Driving all day, we arrived just in time to witness their first game victory on Friday evening. There would be two games the next day, and if they won—the finals would be late Sunday morning.

Saturday dawned with hopes that the team would continue their winning ways. The frivolity of the night before did not hinder their spirits or abilities, as they played superbly in the late-morning game. With time to spare before the four-o'clock contest, parents and coaches huddled around the team and decided it would not only be educational, but very meaningful, for the boys to visit the memorial site of the Alfred P. Murrah Federal Building, which at one time contained offices and a second-floor day care center. On April 19, 1995, one-third of the building was destroyed by a terrorist bomb, killing 168 people—including nineteen children. Hundreds were wounded.

Central to the memorial was a reflecting pool, designed to honor the victims of the horrifying explosion. We stood in silence, feeling emotion, as we imagined the deafening blast, falling concrete and sounds of screams on that fateful morning—at 9:02 a.m. Nineteen artistically-crafted empty chairs had been created and placed on a grassy knoll to represent the children who died. It was a sobering moment for the group of Rebels, putting their lives in perspective—beyond baseball.

The late afternoon game began. They played errorless ball—quite an accomplishment—considering all they had witnessed only two hours earlier. We sat in the top of the bleachers near a couple whose son was pitching for the other team, and was obviously struggling with every throw to maintain his composure. The dad was critical, bellowing loud, non-supportive comments to his son. The mom, on the other hand, to shore-up her son's confidence, shouted,

"You're OK...keep trying...you can do it!"

In an effort to make sure his disparaging language was being heard by his young son out on the mound, the dad moved from the top of the bleachers to the first row. Spitefully, he continued his chants—pitch after pitch,

"Throw strikes! Throw strikes! Come on, what's wrong with you! Throw strikes!"

As he drew a breath from his continuous badgering, the young boy's mom—still sitting at the top of the bleachers— shouted down at her husband.

"He knows he is supposed to throw strikes! He knows that! That's what he is trying to do! What he needs from you is to stop yelling at him and to teach him HOW to throw strikes!"

A memorable weekend, full of emotion...

"Let me tell you a story..."

HARBORING A FUGITIVE

I was sitting in my church office, located near the front entrance to the Sanctuary and the front door. I was quite accessible. Running toward my open door was a young man—out of breath, with sweat dripping from his brow. Speaking very rapidly, he whispered,

"I need to hide here for a few minutes."

We hurriedly ducked into my office.

"Please close the door!"

His name was Brad.

As Paul Harvey used to say so notably,

"And now, the rest of the story."

Let us flash back to my first Sunday in Belle Plaine, Kansas, a tiny bedroom community, just twenty-three miles south of Wichita. The anticipation of this initial Sunday morning—greeting curious parishioners and preaching my first message of faith—made for a very restless night's sleep. Earlier in the evening, I had driven the mile north on the desolate, dimly-lit street which led to the church building and the empty sanctuary. Locking the door behind me and turning on all the lights to give an impression of comforting brightness, I took my place behind a rather large pulpit. I began preaching with gestured animation to the fantasy congregation. It was a needed dress rehearsal. Satisfied with my preparation, I returned to our new home an hour later, parking my Volkswagen Bug in the driveway near the garage.

I woke up to the rhythmic drizzle of a soft summer rain. The time had come to greet the new day. My preparations had been done. The outcome was to be determined. My stomach was churning. Closing the front door, I walked toward my little car. It was no longer parked near the garage, but was now crookedly straddling the driveway near the street. The door was open, and red and green interior lights were flashing on the dashboard. The floor mats were muddy and strewn with wet strands of straw. A stale, revolting aroma greeted me as I leaned in to further examine the harm to my lone, unsuspecting vehicle.

I called the local law enforcement officer. He came over, examined the aftermath of the apparent joyride, and said confidently,

"I'll get right on it!"

At that moment I felt pacified. He gave me a ride to the church.

We now fast-forward to three years later. It is my last Sunday at the church. A congregation of five hundred faithful has grappled theologically in their search for the truth under the leadership of a young pastor. As much as I welcomed my first Sunday three years earlier, I dreaded this day just as much. With tears and smiles, it was my last time to interpret the Gospel of love.

I greeted and hugged many folks that morning. Even though we spoke polite words that seemed to help us through the goodbyes, most of us knew there would be a slim chance our paths would cross again. We all were better folks for having been in an authentic relationship with one another. I walked out of the Sanctuary doors for the last time.

Moving toward our car I sent a prayer of gratitude out into the Universe. My meditative state was abruptly interrupted by the sound of footsteps behind me. It was Brad. My memory of our shared encounter resurfaced with imposing clarity.

Several years earlier, as Brad cowered out of sight, I surreptitiously pulled down a slat of the window shade only to see four men in suits intently approaching the church building. Unexpectedly they turned and left. Closing the shade, I remembered asking Brad what he had done. It was a ritual for him to hide twice a day by the corner of the church, especially in the summer time, and throw rocks at train cars as they passed by the north side of the building. His actions were a destruction of property, and he had finally been reported by the train conductor.

As I continued to look at him, more memories flashed into my awareness. On that traumatic day we had discussed the consequences of his behavior. He told me,

"I'll never throw rocks at the train again. Thanks for letting me hide out."

There was more on this last Sunday he needed to say besides recounting his hiding in my office as a fugitive on the run. With head down and words struggling to be spoken, he said,

"I need to confess something to you. I was the one who took your VW out of your driveway the first Sunday you were here. I stole some beer from a liquor store, took a buddy with me, and we drove crazy through lots of different muddy fields. We were really reckless. I am very sorry. Please forgive me."

That moment seemed like an eternity, standing on that warm sidewalk leading to my refurbished VW. I looked directly at Brad, then back at the church building for the last time. I found the sounds of the chimes quite prophetically well-timed. "What A Friend We Have in Jesus" was broadcasting out into the community. I stared into the sky as if looking for a word or two that might offer a sense of closure for this tender moment. There was only one thing to say that made any sense.

"Brad, I forgive you—I forgive you."

We hugged and went our separate ways.

AN OLDT MENNONITE ADAGE

I never understood my soft-spoken Grandma on Dad's side of the family. They were all Mennonite and spoke Plautdietsch or Low German. English was their second language. Grandma never learned the English language. However, her sweet expression of love, radiating from her eyes and those pink smiling cheeks. was unmistakable.

There were two predictable phenomena I experienced every time we visited Grandma. First, we would eat homemade ice cream. What an unbelievable treat on a hot summer day. It was bountiful, silky smooth and rich as the crown jewels. Secondly, I would spend an unusual amount of time gazing at words in bold print, roughly framed and hanging on Grandma's dining room wall. I would read and reread them, hoping their meaning would leap into my unsophisticated mind. They said:

VE GROW TOO SOON OLDT
UNDT TOO LATE SCHMART.

The truth is, none of us can stop the aging process. Ah, but the rest of the oldt German Mennonite wisdom invites us to nurture our schmarts along the journey.

"Let me tell you a story..."

SORRY ABOUT MY GENETICS

I'm not overly eager to attend any of my high school reunions. The opportunities seemed to loom every year. As I sauntered to the mailbox seventy-five yards down my neighborhood street, I gathered the letters and myriad advertisements. Immediately my eyes noticed the return address in the upper left corner of a thick, bulky envelope. I knew what was inside.

Five years ago, a similar mailing found its way into my mailbox. It was another invitation enticing me to Save The Date for my class gathering—a planned occasion to stare and glare with unmentioned curiosity at past classmates; act like we remember one another, and enter into the rituals of predictable language and niceties. "How have you been?", or "Sure nice to see you!", or "Where are you living these days?"

One year, bravery won the battle, and rather reluctantly, I returned my 35th year high school reunion affirmation card stating I would attend. Not sure what motivated my decision. I had missed all reunions in the past, throwing away invitation after invitation with confidence and glee regarding my decision. I never looked back—except this particular year. Maybe the day I opened that thickly-packed envelope the stars were aligned and the heavens spoke an inexplicable command—"Go!" Or, maybe the invitation from my Mom to have a luncheon at her apartment during the reunion for some of my school buddies was all the motivation I needed.

Eight of us gathered in her cramped, but well-appointed eating space on this warm, humid summer day. If nothing else more dramatic would have occurred for the reunion weekend, this special time of reminiscing was more than sufficient. My youngest daughter, Mary Beth, was home from college, so she assisted Mom in creating a down-home ambiance. With a lovingly-prepared bounty of food and Mom's favorite drink—"Folgers in your cup"—we ate gratefully and shared stories that seemed to have the same introduction, "Do you remember...?"

One of my good friends, John, lived one block from my house. Each day after school, I would coerce or bribe him to help me do my math assignment. That is not an accurate assessment of our times together. Truth is, I asked him to do all my homework. Many times, and quite visibly disgusted, he reluctantly complied. Algebra was a foreign language to me, and I certainly had no desire to understand how mathematic concepts have any application in the world. John eventually taught at Yale.

As Mary Beth leaned over John's shoulder to pour another cup of delicious coffee, he looked at her and cheerfully asked,

"Where are you in college?"

She politely answered,

"I go to Kansas University. I'm getting ready to enter my Junior year." As coffee poured out of the beautiful clay pitcher, the conversation continued.

"Do you like K.U.?"

Mary Beth spoke an emphatic "Yes!"

I listened to them converse with a sense of a father's pride, and appreciated her connecting with one of my dear friends. Then came the memorable question, which to this day reminds me of who I am, what I am, and how I got to be like I am.

"So, Mary Beth, how do you do in math?", John asked, with a touch of sarcasm.

With a wry smile, containing a slight bit of embarrassment, she replied,

"Not too great."

At this moment John looked straight at me with thirty-five-year-old tutorial memories crossing his genius mind, then slowly returned his gaze to Mary Beth, and said profoundly,

"You should have applied for a genetic waiver!"

"Let me tell you a story..."

THE GREATEST YEARS OF MY LIFE

"Those were the greatest years of my life."

These words were spoken with flashes of exciting memories, his eyes bouncing from side to side picturing seven decades of life during the Great Depression and impending second world war. Seems like an oxymoron, but not to my Dad, Jake Dalke. He bid farewell to his earthly life over 20 years ago, but today his spirit has engaged my spirit, and we remember together.

As I drive east from the majestic Colorado mountains towards the western plains of Kansas, with its waving wheat and sounds of combines and tractors tending to the good earth, I reintroduce myself to my Dad. The precious memories are in the deepest recesses of my being. I hear him speaking of the 1930s. I look at the empty passenger car seat and picture him now as a 73-year-old man with a keen mind and a failing body.

His shoulders are slumped and he walks with a slight limp—the preamble to a hip replacement. Silver streaks plentifully complimented his thinning brown hair, adding to his tanned and ruddy complexion. He still has the sturdy look of a farm boy with an infectious smile that causes his blue eyes to crinkle. His strong religious convictions and values have never waned. He is openly patriotic—even though he speaks with a pronounced German brogue—having had minimal exposure to the English language until his elementary school years. I shake my head back and forth as I re-enter the present moment.

I continue to remember—with deep affection and admiration—Dad recounting those seven years in St. John, Kansas. He had applied for a teaching position as the Professor of Music. Truth be known, even allowing his name to be considered before the school board was a toss-up between faith and foolhardiness. Articles in the St. John News were full of doom and gloom. Townsfolk were reeling from some of the most devasting years in the history of this little community of two thousand. A few years before Dad's arrival, the stock market had crashed, wiping out whole fortunes. Banks failed without warning. Crops withered. Dust storms were blinding. Unemployment was rampant. Racism was tolerated. Many folks were dreadfully undernourished and emotionally depleted. His old beat-up Ford rambled into this town. The interview proceeded in a crowded room on the first floor of a rustic, red brick school building.

Two hours later, after energetic sparring between several members of the school board, the position of Professor of Music was offered to Jake. However, there was one curiosity he needed satisfied—seemed like an obvious question with a predictable answer.

"Before I say yes to your kind offer, let me ask how many students do you have in your band?"

There was embarrassing silence. The Superintendent of Schools sheepishly replied:

Well, Jake, we don't have a band. Oh, one of our young ladies plays her grandpa's saxophone, but that's it. Now you know why we want to hire you—to develop a band. We need someone like you to lift our spirits. Our town is dying. We have very little to count on. Maybe a sermon or two on Sundays gives us a temporary boost. We want to laugh and hope that life is worth living. We believe—no, we seriously believe— that maybe, just maybe, music might be the medicine we need. Are you up for it?

Instruments were ordered from a music store fifty miles away. It was a taste of Christmas, as wannabe musicians gleefully unloaded the truck, claiming certain instruments for themselves. Jake began giving lessons to the eager youth. Before long, squeaks from reed instruments and blurted sounds from brass horns morphed into mellow tones. A band was born.

In three years' time seventy boys and girls donned their blue and white uniforms to march and play at state fairs, small town parades and half-time performances during high school football games. Mom lovingly packed lunches for Cleo and Joanna, two African-American youth, often not allowed at restaurants with the rest of their classmates. Music was beginning to instill a sense of hope into the lives of a "down-and-out" town—even as the country's economic depression lingered. The buzz on the street was cheerful, not mournful.

In 1938, four years after Dad's arrival, the now-ninety-member band entered a state music contest. Preparation for precise marching routines and a required symphonic composition required many hours of dedicated practice before and after school, in the evenings and on weekends.

They met the challenge and won first in the state competition. This honor qualified them for the district contest. First place again. Onward to the National Band Festival in Omaha, Nebraska. The mantra on the lips of the townsfolk was "Isn't our band just wonderful?" Yes, they claimed the band as their own.

Omaha was a shot of reality for the band. They placed second in both marching and concert, and did not make the cut in the sight-reading portion of the competition. The results propelled Jake and his budding musicians to rededicate themselves musically for the next year. So, in 1939, at the National Band contest in Denver, Colorado, the now confident performers astounded the judges initially with their marching precision and then with their wonderfully-blended musicianship on the concert stage. With tears of joy, Jake called in the results to the St. John News. The next day a caravan of cars met the band fifty miles from St. John and honked the buses home to a crowded gathering of banner-waving parents and friends.

The following year in a newly-selected city, Jake's Band once again swept the competition at the National Band Convention in Kansas City, Missouri.

Through the years, these eight words would find a place in our family conversations: "Those were the greatest years of my life!"

Many years later I decided to unearth the reasons those words were spoken so often. I waved goodbye to the mountains and greeted the Kansas plains, with my Dad's spirit by my side. I went to St. John for three days like an explorer seeking a treasure. I listened to ten seventy-year-old former band members relive those years as adolescents playing in "Mr. Dalke's Band". They spoke of feeling inspired in finding a sense of purpose as teenagers through music. In unison, I heard them say, "Yes, those were the best years of our lives, too."

The owner of the St. John newspaper gave me a key to the archives where I read every article about the band from 1934 to 1940. I vicariously heard the ethereal musical renderings of Lenore, Bill, Jimmy and Waneta. I felt the comforting presence of my parents' spirits, as I pictured how they brought new life to a lifeless little town through the miracle of music.

I returned home imagining sounds of John Phillip Sousa's marches pounding their beats on the pavement. With eagerness I had not felt before, I thumbed through Dad's tattered, yellowish-paged scrapbook of what he deemed important about his band. It had not been easy for him. He left the farm to follow his dream of teaching music, choral and instrumental. He left the street corners of neighboring Mennonite farm settlements where he and his siblings would witness about their faith through music and word. He left a little farm community where everyone knew one another for a world where he knew no one. In a faithful gesture, he reached out, and a group of school board members said, "We need you."

There is a postscript of truth to this story. Talent and ingenuity are extremely important, but they do not stand alone. Dad valued relationships. The wisdom he gained— from harvesting the wheat with his parents and siblings on blistering hot days; from appreciating life's simplest of blessings; from pulling together as a large family amidst sad moments and meager celebrations of joy; and from never missing the opportunity to speak words of kindness and appreciation to others—was Jake at his core.

There was no entitlement in Jake's Band. He insisted on respect for one another's differences and unique abilities. More than anything, he invited young people to feel a deep sense of passion for the beauty of music.

Now we know why "Those were the greatest years of my life!"

"Let me tell you a story..."

MORE THAN DIRT

It was almost her dying breath—and these, her last words.
Mom laboriously whispered to my sister Judy and me,

"Just have fun with the land."

I was never told why my grandparents purchased eighty
acres of undeveloped land in Western Kansas around the
time of the depression. Folks were losing money, not
spending it. The land was over 100 miles from their home.
They were not farmers. It seemed like Grandma's calling was
to cook unbelievable meals whose smells tantalized the
neighbors and welcomed Grandpa home from managing his
hardware store. Not sure they had an ounce of farm-blood in
them. Doesn't really matter. They just trusted Orville Jones,
a local farmer and friend, to till the ground and they would
pray for rain and an abundant wheat crop. Years passed.
They must have given the same farewell speech to Mom and
my Aunt Ruth, "Just have fun with the land." It was, and is, a
loving legacy.

From her death bed, Mom graciously willed the plot of
earth to us. Orville—whom she said was a "tall drink of
water"—passed the caretaking of the land to his son, Jim.
Folks in the county describe him as a "very good farmer."
Each year during the month of June, I make my annual

telephone call to our Western Kansas Co-Op. Their silos reach to the heavens—and in them is stored our wheat. Our land will have spoken—either with a whimper or a standing ovation.

A few years ago, before Judy's illness consumed her body, she flew to Denver, where Sheryl and I met her. From there we drove six hours into the wide-open spaces, guided each mile by rays of warm sunshine. Eventually we arrived at our eighty acres of dirt—God's dirt.

"There it is," said Jim. "Your Grandpa and Grandma believed in this land. And now it is yours."

We just stared. No words were spoken. I leaned down and picked up a clod that had not been plowed under. I held it to the expansive sky in a gesture of gratitude to the Creator of heaven and earth.

In the hectic, rushing moments of our everyday turmoils and joys, we must not lose sight of the potential contained in a simple handful of dirt that grounds us and says to *be thankful for your past, be very present in the now, and trust in the goodness that is meant to be.*

AUTUMN

A THOUGHTFUL QUESTION

There are beneficent mortals in our lives that just know how to ask the right question, firmly and lovingly. Carter Barker was one such creature.

In the mid-1960's I served on the staff of Pratt First United Methodist Church in a midwestern Kansas community endowed with many wonderfully-caring folks. The town was welcoming with its wide brick streets, bordered with retail vendors and private shopkeepers that kept the residents adequately supplied for their physical needs. There were several churches sprinkled on corners throughout the town, plus four elementary schools, two middle schools, and one high school. One week a year, the community rolled out the red carpet for nervous, hopeful contestants and their staunchly-supportive sponsors as they invaded the city community building for the Ms. Kansas Pageant.

For five exuberant years my friendships in Pratt blossomed and grew as I immersed myself in relationships and constant activities, particularly in the high school. In 1968, the year after I left, my dear friend, Jim Lewis (the coach of the Pratt High School football team) had an undefeated season, won first place in the state playoffs and was chosen the State High School Coach of the Year by his peers.

It is now fifty years later. Jim is retired and living alone outside of town near the Pratt Country Club golf course. Many of the youthful players who garnered the unbelievable State Championship trophy have moved away as their local employment opportunities declined. Nevertheless, although small in number, the current high school band is powerful in their musical expression, and the football team continues to play their hearts out, much like fifty years ago.

My telephone rang. I noticed on my caller ID it was Carter Barker, my long-lasting buddy of years ago. He would sit in the first row of the church balcony and subtly wave at me as I sat on the chancel platform portraying thoughtful reverence. His voice had not changed. There was a slight southern accent as he started the conversation, addressing me as he always did with humor and slow rumbling utterances.

"Deacon Dave...now I want you to listen carefully to what I'm saying."

Becoming intense and with a sense of urgency, he continued,

"Pratt High School is honoring your close friend Jim Lewis at the football game on October 13. I'm sure you remember it was fifty years ago he coached an undefeated team and some of those players—who were in your Methodist Youth Fellowship (MYF) group—are returning to celebrate that great team and honor Jim."

He paused, maybe for emphasis or just to take a deep breath before planting the clincher question:

"Now, Deacon Dave, can you tell me any good reason you can't be here to help honor your good friend, Jim?"

My life was put on hold as I mulled over Carter's question.

Jim would invite me to join the team in the pungent, aromatic locker room before each home game to pray for the wisdom to play with a clear head and safety for themselves and their opponents. I had been very close to many of the players of yesteryear. Those were moments never to be forgotten.

To go back would be a nine-hour drive. Selfishly, it could be a time of renewal for me with many lasting memories. Our daughter Julie was born there with little chance to survive at two pounds and eleven ounces. I remember sitting alone on the hill in the end zone watching the football team play as I tearfully contemplated the possibility of still losing a spouse and a firstborn from an unexpected traumatic birth four days earlier. To this day, the Pratt community still takes credit for praying Julie into the world.

As thoughts and feelings kicked up inside, I pondered Carter's question. *Can you tell me any reason...?*

On this beautiful fall evening I took my place on the old, wooden bleachers. They were just as I remembered them. It was always wise to take a blanket to cover the splintered surface. Tonight, I felt an unexplainable warmth in my belly to see many of the team members and their coaches of fifty years ago walk onto the field at half time to be recognized amidst the happy applause of the crowd. For alumni, their cheers were born out of pride and memories. For others with graying hair and receding hairlines, there was an internal celebration. They remembered... I felt tears rolling down my cold cheeks.

After a hard-fought victory the High School band performed. The crowd, out of courtesy and expectation, stayed to listen. The band had yielded their half-time presentation to the heart-warming festivities of fifty years ago. They played their very difficult pieces from memory, with marching routines that had the crowd on their feet. My tears continued to roll. I witnessed a most sensitive moment of respect as the football team—still in stained jerseys of victory—knelt in the end zone for the full performance, to support the band.

I went to Jim's home later that night. Many of "his" team were there, plus past students and MYF-ers who had made the trip to their old haunts of fifty years ago. We hugged our history, thanking one another for being in each other's lives at such a memorable time. We all had changed but had not forgotten. In those brief moments sitting in Jim's welcoming living room, some of us were transported back to the church to a Sunday night Methodist Youth Fellowship meeting, or to being at a Work Camp in Montana, or just having a planning session after school. We were part of each other's lives once again.

None of those feelings would have been resurrected if my good friend, Carter, had not called and said,

"Deacon Dave, can you tell me any good reason you can't be here to honor your good friend, Jim?"

I couldn't think of one.

"Let me tell you a story..."

THE STATEMENT

Ever since she was six years old I had taken our daughter, Mary Beth, to gymnastics lessons. There were many years of sore muscles, bruises and tears as she developed strength and flexibility in her arms, legs and abdominal muscles. And then the payoff. Rubbing excess chalk from her hands, she would wait for the judges to nod her way. With permission granted, she would be hoisted onto the uneven bars to begin her routine, or she would run at break-neck speed to launch herself, twisting airborne over the imposing vault, or coordinate her agility on the mat with music during her floor exercise, or finesse acrobatic moves in the air while landing with precise balance on a four-inch beam.

An essential part of her training was her weekly ballet class. As I watched from the periphery of the room full of mounted bars, mirrors and shiny wooden floors, my eyes would lock into the quiet and dramatic techniques of training one's body. I wondered how difficult ballet could be. I had athletic skills. I had some agility. I had good eye-hand coordination. I was teachable.

An adult class was formed with some of my more adventurous friends. We hired a knowledgeable, even-

tempered ballet instructor—one that we assumed would have
tolerance for six budding Mikhail Baryshnikovs.

Each class began by warming up our bodies with
stretching exercises. We would tightly grip the supportive
bars with grunts and groans as pleasant music softly
enveloped the room. Skittish and watchful, we listened
closely to commands which were given to us in French. Our
instructor would roam the room correcting our body
positions, loud enough for all to hear. My learning curve was
suspect. I knew the term "pirouette", but the simple turn was
not simple. My "plié" pose created not only pain but crackling
and popping noises as I asked my knees to bend with suavity
and elegance.

The lessons continued and each week's story was
recounted colorfully to Mary Beth. Always sympathetic, she
reacted with a wry smile.

One evening, our instructor's booming announcement
created a rumbling of apprehension in every one of us.

"Tonight, we will learn an *arabesque* and a *ciseaux*." I
thought: *who in the deepest recesses of their soul ever suggested
taking this class?* He demonstrated with fluent ease the
arabesque, extending one of his legs horizontally backward
and his body leaning forward, with his arms outstretched. I
wobbled in my attempt, ever thankful for the bar I was
grasping. Realizing the ineptness of his subjects, our tutor
(who was not being compensated nearly enough) moved
forward to the next ballet position. He placed a large pillow
in the middle of the room.

"I want everyone to line up in one corner. You will run to
the opposite side of the room, jumping over the pillow doing
a split in the air, one leg in front of your body and the other
one behind. Got it?"

To relive the rest of this story is a reiteration of mental agony. That cataclysmic evening, I made the fateful decision to be the first to sail over the pillow in a *ciseaux* position. Attempt number one drew no praise.

"No...no!" shouted the instructor. "Try it again."

I returned to my corner of the room, took a deep breath, and charged the pillow—determined to fly over it with ease and suppleness.

"No...no...go again!"

The words cut a swath of fear wider than a combine in a wheat field. I stared at the pillow. I wanted to go home. I wanted to quit this class.

Every inadequate feeling I had experienced from childhood to this dramatically-breathtaking moment came roaring into my being. Without hesitation, I bolted towards the object that had "grown" to an insurmountable height, like the raked-up pile of fallen leaves outside the studio door. Unfortunately, I repeated my prior feeble attempts. Returning to the group, emphatic words filled the silence of the room. Looking directly at me, our instructor merely said,

"David, all I want you to do is make a statement with your body."

"Let me tell you a story..."

DON'T MISS IT

My eyes gazed at the brightly-colored numbers on the alarm clock, then at the ceiling fan, twirling and purring in the shadows of our bedroom. It was 3:30 in the morning. This night, sleep had not been my constant companion. Next to me, Sheryl continued her rhythmic breathing. I carefully rehearsed how not to disturb her. She has two cancers. Sleep is her treatment.

In the reverence of the stillness I heard this soft, gentle voice.

"What shall we do?"

Gathering my hazy thoughts, I responded,

"Sorry, I thought you were asleep."

She turned to face me. I could barely see the outline of her face but her words were becoming more audible and persuasive. They flowed like a rippling mountain stream surrounded by darkness as she gained momentum from slumber to alert consciousness.

"If you're not sleepy, let's go somewhere."

Once again, I glanced at the numbers on the bedside timepiece.

"Sheryl, it is 3:45 a.m."

"I know," she said with an elevated voice.

"Come on, it will be fun!"

Some of the most captivating times in my life have been those moments that make the least amount of sense. This was one of them. I slowly crawled out from under three comforting, warm blankets. As my feet touched the floor, something clicked inside of me. My blurry brain jumped into clarity, and my feelings had a sensation of excitement. *Yes,* I said to myself, *this sounds like an adventure.*

We began aimlessly driving around. Houses were eerily dark. Only the tall street lights guided our path. When my Dad died, street lights blinked at me as though he was sending a message that "all is okay." That night, we noticed one faded out and then gradually came back on. Maybe Dad was blessing this odyssey into the unknown. We kept driving and searching for our yet-to-be-discovered destination. Then it appeared—a newly-built, twenty-four-hour discount giant, with not one car in the smoothly-paved parking lot. This was our moment.

Hand in hand, we approached the automatic front doors. They slowly opened. Then the most amazing thing happened to us. We walked in, only to have an energetic, smiling, elderly woman in a gold and blue vest, loudly proclaim,

"Welcome to Walmart!"

It was four a.m. The sun had not made its appearance over the eastern horizon. Other than the early-rising, blue-vested folks stocking the shelves, we were the only ones in this store. She continued,

"Here, each of you take a cart. You can race each other!"

There was something contagious about this happily-employed woman. We talked later about how much we admired her undeniably cheerful spirit. Some human beings just seem glad to be here in this world. She was one of them.

We maneuvered our empty carts up one stark aisle and down another, apologizing to those folks on their knees placing newly-arrived products on the shelves. We thanked them for their toiling all night. They smiled and muttered the obligatory,

"Have a nice day."

It had just begun. Our conversation drifted from "Seems like we should buy something" to "Where shall we go next?"

I can't remember what we purchased that early morning. We wandered into the still-empty parking lot as the sun began to peek over the autumn-colored trees of the city. Silence on the roads was giving way to the rumbling sounds of cars and trucks. For many early risers, it was their moment to greet the new day. For us, it was time to have breakfast and go back to bed. We sat in a café with smells of Folgers coffee and sizzling eggs tantalizing our senses. I thought to myself: *life is so full of schedules and obligations, and playfulness is often just a reward for good work.* But this moment was not one of them, and it doesn't usually have to make sense.

Don't miss it!

A Delayed Note Of Gratefulness

He was my inspiration and friend. Every Sunday, I would sit enthralled in the balcony's front row of our ornate, Gothic sanctuary and listen to him paint life's pictures with his gestures and haunting vocal inflections. He made the ordinary into the extraordinary. An airport was not just a place where planes landed. Ron called it "...aprons of asphalt bleeding into fields and waiting for skybirds to come home to their nesting."

Ron and Ethel lived on a ranch fifty miles west of Wichita. He cherished walks on his land, especially in the late summer and early fall. He would say,

"I raise registered quarter horse colts and ordinary kids."

Often his stories would reflect how important it is for all of us to savor the precious moments of our creation. Every Sunday he would remind us we have only a brief period of time to shout a loud "Yes" to our Creator and the paths we walk, from the rising of the sun to the greeting of the stars. This is our time.

My life hurried by, but not without memorable chats between the two of us. I cherished every word, every ounce of wisdom. When life seemed mundane or without purpose,

I would open up my memory bank and make a life-sustaining withdrawal.

One evening—in the late '80s, I had a call from my Dad telling me Ron had broken his leg and was in the hospital. Living a prohibitive distance for visiting him, I decided to write him a note. There must be no more waiting, not another procrastinated second, to tell him how much I treasured our relationship. My intentions were noble. Yet, fleeting days turned into months and I had not put the pen to the paper. But we can only be chastised by our conscience so long before it drives us to action. No more delay—I began to write my note of gratefulness.

Some days later, I received a note from Ron's wife, Ethel. It read:

> I wanted you to know that although your cheery
> message arrived just after Ron's passing, we thank
> you for caring enough to feel compelled to
> encourage him. He thought so much of you, David,
> and was always interested in what you were doing.

I mailed my note to him on Thursday. Ron never received it. He died on Friday.

"Let me tell you a story..."

UNDER THE BRIM

My parents raised my sister and me to have a strong work ethic. Hours were spent at the dinner table listening to Dad regale us with tales about his life on the farm as a young boy, doing early morning chores and helping in harvest under noon's blistering sun until midnight's twinkling stars. Mom would chime in with her stories of cleaning the house exquisitely and never complaining about the errands on her neatly prepared list. Work, at home and outside our home, was not only expected, but was our identity.

In one of our special times of sharing I asked my sister,

"Judy, when you were in Junior High School, did anyone ever ask you what you were going to be when you grew up?"

Without hesitation, she answered,

"No, I was never asked that question, because everyone already knew what I was going to be—either a nurse, flight attendant, secretary, or teacher. And it had to be an elementary school teacher!"

Then she said,

"What about you?"

Of course, I wanted to be a sports announcer and travel with the St. Louis Cardinals baseball team, and live in a hotel so I wouldn't have to make my bed. The truth was, no matter how I entered into the world of the employed I knew I would need to make an impact. Make a difference. A subtle message bestowed on me by loving parents and those who asked, "David, what are you going to be when you grow up?"

Unbeknownst to me I began building a resumé, which included my varied work experiences. In junior high I weeded gardens, mowed lawns and had three paper routes (one in the morning and two in the evening), all at the same time. During high school I drove a Coca-Cola delivery truck after school and on Saturdays. I loved having a chauffeur's license, even though it was a requirement. I spoke of it often, especially to my buddies.

Then came college. I wanted to have fun, earn some money, and study, in that order. I started traversing the downtown streets, with my prepared speech about being a college student who wanted part time work that would fit my class schedule. I practiced the words over and over, as I went from one store to another. Then it happened. I found myself standing under a large protruding sign that said *Spines Department Store.* I did an about-face, and found myself gazing at several mannequins, dressed in three-piece suits, spit-shined shoes and gentlemen's hats, with each brim finely tilted at a downward angle. In an opposite window were stylishly-dressed women mannequins with well-coiffed hair, purses draped over shoulders, looking into the lights. I thought, *Now, I could work here!*

I entered Spines Department Store. I noticed a nattily-dressed young man standing behind one of the glass counters, folding fine handkerchiefs. At precisely the same moment, we made eye contact. He smiled. We introduced ourselves. I felt a momentary rush of adrenalin and courage to ask my question.

"Is there someone I could talk to about working here?"

He continued folding.

"So, you are looking for a job?"

I nodded my head up and down. My Dad and Mom had schooled me in the protocols of how I should dress when applying for a job. I looked the part.

"Are you in college?" he inquired.

"Yes, and I am right in the middle of setting my schedule of classes, so I could be flexible in my hours here."

I hoped that was true. There was a brief pause. My eyes darted downward at the lighted case full of men's accessories. I thought, *I can fold handkerchiefs and arrange ties.* I casually looked up and noticed his name tag which read, "Assistant Manager." Words ricocheted across the counter, and then,

"When can you start?"

My college experience working at Spines was more than rewarding. I immersed myself in every aspect of the clothing business. I could sell. However, it was very unwise for me to cross the invisible line from men's accessories to suits, slacks and sport coats. That domain belonged to two very knowledgeable and experienced middle-aged men who worked on commission. My place was at the front of the store, where I shared space with William, a seventy-five-year-old man, who used to sell suits in the back of the store, but now had been relegated to the front. There he greeted shoppers and sold everything except suits, of course.

One of William's specialties was selling men's hats. His case was full of beautiful, wide-brimmed, stylish headwear. Day after day I would watch him delicately place a felt hat on the glass counter, stroking the brim with his aged, but nimble, fingers. He treated it like a newborn baby. Then, in slow motion, he would meticulously invert the hat so the insides would face the customer. Then I would hear him say,

"What do you think? Isn't it beautiful?"

One day I moseyed over to William's counter and asked him why he showed hats with such grace and style to every customer. He gently brought a hat from inside the case and placed it on the glass:

Notice the structure and style, the color, and the
width of the headband that is supported by the brim.
That is what a person sees. But what sells this hat is
not what is on the outside and visible. It is what is on
the inside, under the brim—the silk and other
materials of substance. That is what gives this hat
character.

Then he paused and slowly repositioned the hat, delicately grasping the brim, and placing it in the lighted glass case, and said,

"This hat is like us. Our beauty is on the inside, but too often, all some folks notice is the outside."

NEVER HAD TO SAY

The two-storied, gray wooden house sat stately on the corner directly across from the grade school building. Several chairs were placed on the spacious front porch, welcoming all who wanted to visit or just watch cars go by ever so slowly on a summer evening, a frequent pastime in this small Kansas town. Uncle Fred and Aunt Eula had lived in this place for nearly forty years.

Fred Howard was the local pharmacist and owned Howard Drug. He was a trusted medical professional. Bottles of prescribed drugs sat on the shelves in the back of his store, out of the reach of everyone except my Great Uncle Fred. Once in a while, he would emerge from his pill-counting and come to the front of the store to pour himself a frosty Coca-Cola, or to stir up a mouth-watering cherry malt, with luscious Steffens ice cream, just for me. When visiting my Grandpa and Grandma, who lived just two blocks away, I would spend countless hours at Uncle Fred's drugstore.

Aunt Eula was the most benevolent person I have ever known. If my mom complimented her on a piece of furniture or knick-knack, she would simply say with the graciousness of an empress,

"Here, Katherine, why don't you take it?"

She loved to cook and her food preparation was presented simply and beautifully. Every conversation with her left little doubt about what she believed spiritually, how she felt about her town, and what she thought about the status of current affairs. No one had ever been created like her, nor ever would be again.

I remember the day Aunt Eula drew her final breath on this earth. I received an unexpected telephone call from my cousin Kent.

"David, Aunt Eula died last night. They want you to come and speak at her service."

As I drove the hundred miles to a grieving family and community, I rehearsed in my mind the meager declarations I had prepared for the eulogy. The combination of words and thoughts seemed woefully powerless. She was more than words.

We would be celebrating her life in the same Methodist Church where my parents had been married thirty years before. Many of the folks that attended that sweltering summer wedding, with sweaty smiles adorning their faces, were now shedding tears. On this crisp fall day the choir sang with quivering voices without Aunt Eula's ever-present soprano vibrato. Kent offered a measure of hope as he read haltingly from the Scriptures:

"The Lord...the Lord is my Shepherd, I shall not..."

I was next. I do not remember the words that came out of me that day.

Kent had flown in from the West Coast and needed my help with transportation to the airport. As we rode together, many memories of Aunt Eula flooded the car. It was a time of catharsis for both of us. When we neared the airport, Kent thanked me for the two-hour ride and conversation. Then— as if he had been savoring one last truth—he said,

"You know, David, Aunt Eula never had to say, 'I wished I would've...' "

A FUN SPINNING MACHINE

Someone once said, "The best of friends are two people who dislike the same person." However, the best of friends just might be two people who like the sound of spinning malt machines.

It was advertised as a "Spectacular Late Summer/Early Fall, Never-To-Be-Missed Sale." I slowly meandered up and down the aisles of elongated tables full of well-used and antiquated restaurant supplies—all priced for sale. The owners were also sadly saying goodbye to thirty-five years of welcoming repeat customers and weary travelers to their laminated, plastic-covered tables full of delicious homemade food. I greeted the teary couple as they spoke futuristically of planned dream vacations and uninterrupted trips to spend leisure time with their four grandchildren. My energy towards them was layered with compassion. I thanked them for providing an ambience of comfort and friendliness for the multitude of hungry souls they had greeted through the years. As we visited, I found myself shading my eyes from a disturbing and blinding glare of sunshine—bouncing off a metal machine—labeled "Make An Offer." Little did I know, the distraction would propel me towards fulfilling one of my unmet fantasies.

I noticed other antique explorers and disguised restaurant dealers eyeing this statuesque, light green, ten-pound Hamilton Beach spinner. It was a vintage, yet fully functional, malt machine. This had to be mine. I inched with barely-disguised intensity towards my hopeful purchase. As the browsers glanced at a huge set of sparsely chipped dishes, I wrapped my eager hand around the neck of the beautifully-designed apparatus, and immediately walked briskly towards the negotiating table. My childhood fantasy of being the best Malt-Maker in the whole wide world was within reach.

My great uncle Fred was my grandma's brother. He was a pharmacist who owned Howard Drug, located downtown in a small farming community. My grandparents lived only two blocks from his drug store, which was nestled next to Dillon's Food Market. It was very convenient for Grandpa and me to pick up grocery items and then go next door to relax and have a refreshing Coca-Cola. It was a carefree ritual. We were lifelong pals.

As I paid for the well-worn malt machine, I had flashbacks of those moments many years ago—at Uncle Fred's drug store. While Grandpa would sit at an off-white marble table sipping his Coke, I would be glancing across the soda fountain counter—intently observing a smiling young woman filling a silver metal container with three scoops of Steffens vanilla ice cream; two helpings of malt powder; one fourth cup of whole milk; and three energetic plunges of chocolate syrup—all ready to be spun into a delectable, mouth-watering treat. Once in a while, she would ask me if I wanted to come behind the counter and help her mix the ingredients. While my friends were dreaming of being the fastest runners in school, or being stronger than Superman, or even being

President of the United States, I spent my time wanting to own a malt shop with a huge, brightly-colored sign reading:

"World's Fantastic Malts–by David."

Today, on our kitchen counter, tucked against the junction of the adjoining walls, proudly stands a Hamilton Beach malt machine—with three stacked silver containers surrounding its long spinner. It is thought to be a 1951 model—at least that's what I was told by the retiring restaurant owners many years ago. It has never stopped creating fun with its blending magic, always a member of the family that doesn't disappoint. There is joy in its whirling sound and predictable smiles of satisfaction at the first curious taste.

For many years, neighborly conversations or hopeful business deals have been struck over cups of Folger's coffee. But, if you come to our welcoming home, there will be a fun spinning machine to greet you—with whatever flavor tickles your palate. You will be served a special ice-cream treat—a chocolate, cherry or butterscotch malt with corresponding syrup drizzled over the signature decorative dollop of ice cream on top—signaling that you just might be tasting

The   World's   (most)   Fantastic   Malt.

CHURCH CHIMES AT 4:27

It was a beautiful Autumn late afternoon. The sun was on its way down, glowing over the multicolored treetops. Leaves had pulled loose from their fragile stems and had begun to float to earth, twirling and dipping, ballerina-like. A white cross peered into the distance from the steeple. Such was the moment, all elements blending and fitting together as beautifully as a tightly-composed symphony.

Inside the V-shaped red brick building was a medium-sized sanctuary with maroon carpet and comfortable pews—sometimes too comfortable for dozing parishioners. However, this Friday afternoon, sitting alone in the front pew were Cora and Ira. She was eighty-nine years old and he was ninety-two. They were going to be the matron of honor and best man for their dearest friends, soon to be married.

In my office, a few feet from the sanctuary door, sat Bill and Maude for their premarital counseling session. The years had been generous to them, but not to their former spouses. Their love had been shrouded in grief several years ago, but had been reborn, flourishing between the two of them. They had chosen to not invite any of their grown children or grandchildren to their wedding—only Ira and Cora, their very best friends, who sat waiting for them.

In the solemnity of the moment, they sat next to one another, reaching out to hold each other's hands. Bill was ninety years old and Maude had graced this earth for eighty-eight years. I felt so honored to be in their presence.

"There are a couple of questions I have for both of you before we go into the sanctuary and hear you shout a loud *'Yes!'* to one another." They were ready to answer. I continued,

"Our ceremony will be short, simple and full of love. At one point we will have moments of prayer. Do you want to kneel at that time?"

Looking at one another in prolonged silence, Maude then replied,

"Sure, we will kneel."

I continued with a question I had asked many couples in premarital visits.

"After I pronounce you husband and wife, you can kiss one another. Do you want to do that?"

Again, silence. Then Maude spoke up with excitement in her voice.

"Oh yes, we will kiss. He's a great kisser!"

Bill lowered his blushing head. It was now time to leave the office and walk together into the sanctuary. As Bill sauntered through the doorway, Maude turned and touched me tenderly on my arm.

"David, please don't ask us to kneel. We just wanted you to think we could."

My heart laughed as I led them down the aisle to greet Ira and Cora. The four of them stood before me at the altar, facing an open Bible on a draped table and a hanging cross suspended by invisible wires. There were no flowers, no music, no restless and curious observers or photographers—

only Maude and Bill and their closest friends, Ira and Cora. I looked at them with a lump in my throat. After a hard swallow, I began to speak to the sacredness of this moment.

It came time for the placing of the rings on their fingers. Bill had both rings in his pocket. Proudly he held them in the palm of his roughened hand. As I started to take them from him, Ira playfully looked at Bill and said,

"Let me see those rings. Those are beautiful. You really did right by Maude. I bet they cost you a pretty penny!"

There has to be another sacrament in the community of believers. It is flexibility. I had never experienced a two-minute conversation at the altar by a wedding party, let alone by four folks who combined for 359 years.

With tears and a trembling voice, I pronounced them a married couple and invited them to embrace, as only a great kisser could do. At that moment the chimes began to sound, broadcasting their melodious glad tidings for miles around. It was 4:27 in the afternoon. Curiously the chimes were programmed to ring on the hour. I don't try to understand how the Spirit moves in those mysterious ways. I just know at the altar on that late afternoon, something happened that brought us all to our knees.

"Let me tell you a story..."

THE PARABLE OF THE PIZZA DELIVERY

Jesus was a stimulating and captivating story teller. He spoke to the curious and the committed about fruit trees, mustard seeds, wheat, talents, ten bridesmaids, lost sheep and a wedding banquet. Scripture tells us Jesus' spiritual lessons were in the thought-provoking form of parables. When his Disciples questioned why their trusted and humble leader spoke with such stories, Jesus' answer was simple:

"The reason I speak to them in parables is that seeing they do not perceive, and hearing they do not listen, nor do they understand." (Matthew 13:13).

Life is full of stories. Some of them are dramatic. Others are simple, like footsteps on a shell-strewn beach with the sun glistening on the dancing waves. Where life is, there is a story, or a parable. I share one with you now.

Years ago, our oldest daughter and her young family lived in Battle Creek, Michigan. Traditional roles prevailed as Julie gave daily devoted guidance to the three children, while Rich's expertise as a Division Supervisor guided the refurbishing of private airplanes at a plant ten miles away. Once a month, after work, and with a hard-earned pay check in hand, Rich would stop by the family's favorite pizza restaurant and bring home their favorite pie: pepperoni and mushroom. On those days he would receive an unqualified hero's welcome when arriving with a box that stirred all the senses. As the family struggled to place the melted, drooping cheese pieces on their plates, without fail, someone would say,

"This is the best pizza ever!"

Steve's Pizza was a Carry-out Only establishment. No seats—just stand in line, let your taste buds be tantalized, and wait to hear your name.

Twenty-two years later, after several moves to other airplane plants, Rich and Julie settled in Indianapolis, Indiana. Their fantasy of growing old together was abruptly interrupted like a tire exploding on a smooth freeway. His diagnosis was cancer. Immediate surgery and treatment were needed. Month after month, reports spelled out agonizing results. The harrowing disease continued to spread throughout his once hardy, but now withering body. Their hopeful words changed to "What do we still want to do with our lives together?"

With the mournful limitation of time and lamentable loss of energy, they decided to make one last trip, close to home.

"Julie," said Rich, "let's drive to Battle Creek and get a Steve's Pizza. It is only three and one-half hours away."

It was the final dream.

The trip began. Julie drove—but not to Battle Creek, Michigan. Her intuition guided her to the emergency room of the hospital instead. Rich was quickly and carefully admitted to the Intensive Care Unit, and more tests were administered. My telephone rang. A quiet, tearful voice greeted me with these words:

"Dad, the doctor just told us that Rich may only have a few days to live...maybe a couple weeks."

I remembered that plaintive cry from many years ago when she would come home from school and needed a hug or an empathic ear.

"Julie, do you want me to come and be with you?" She said, "Not yet. I'll call you."

As their grown children descended on the once-playful home, now filled with anguish and hurting hearts, my telephone rang again.

"Grandpa, this is Christopher. Please come as soon as you can—tonight, if possible."

The urgency was unmistakable. I arrived at midnight. The flight was cathartic for me, as I sat next to a young woman who inquired about my family. My story unfurled. Her tears gathered and spilled out. Death seemed so out of order. Upon landing, the two of us walked towards the baggage area, scanning for our welcoming families. A grim-faced young man approached me. My young traveling companion said,

"That must be Christopher."

She greeted him with an unexpected hug and with continually-flowing tears, simply said,

"I'm so sorry."

The October night had a head start towards dawn. I waited until the sun peeked into my bedroom before greeting Rich. He had embraced his approaching death with dignity. I walked slowly into his bedroom and leaned down to softly embrace him. With a firm voice he said,

"I want you to do my funeral."

There was only one answer.

The next three weeks were a vigil. Rich taught us all how to die. In reaching out to death calmly, but with wrenching sadness, he anticipated missing his family and not being able to celebrate the forthcoming birth of a new granddaughter. Each time any one of us shared silence or a word or two with him, his parting benediction would be,

"It's going to be OK."

The next few watchful days were a ritual of pacing back and forth from the kitchen to Rich's room. Inventing conversations to ease the reality of his illness were both meaningful and, at times, a tad superficial for all of us. However, one lingering thought hovered over much of the conversations—the sentimental disappointment of not tasting Steve's Pizza in Battle Creek, Michigan—one last time.

Julie curled up next to her fragile husband. As the grandkids continued to sort through the food, so generously given by co-workers, friends and extended family, something unmistakable nudged me upstairs to the telephone. I closed the door and picked up the phone to call Steve's Pizza. A welcoming, youthful voice came on the line.

"I have a special request," I said. "Is there a manager or owner I could speak to?"

A young man named Dalton came to the phone. He was the manager on duty that day. I told him of Rich's and Julie's affinity for Steve's pizza, and the somber reason they could not come to Battle Creek for one last slice. Apologetically I asked,

"Any chance you could just send them a text or email on behalf of Steve's Pizza? I know how much they would appreciate hearing from their favorite pizza parlor."

There was a pause, then Dalton said,

"Give me your phone number. I'll call you back in thirty minutes."

My phone rang louder than usual—just seven minutes later.

"This is Dalton…"

I had meager expectations in contacting Steve's Pizza. No one else in the house knew of my intentions, and yet I kept feeling prodded. I could decipher muffled voices downstairs with a smattering of laughter, easing the hovering grief. I was hoping some kind gesture from Steve's Pizza might offer a temporary panacea amidst the tears and reality of the moment. What I heard from Dalton was beyond my expectation.

"David, what kind of pizza does Rich's family like?"

I replied, "Please hold, I'll ask the kids."

The answer was pepperoni and mushroom. But, why ask? The unexpected and astonishing answer came as Dalton continued.

"I'll put two large pizzas in the oven just before I close at 10:30. I'll be happy to bring them to you."

I fumbled for the right words. Clarity was of the essence.

"Dalton, I'm not sure I am being clear. I am calling you from Indianapolis. That is 220 miles from Battle Creek—a three-and one-half-hour drive in each direction."

I then reiterated.

"Listen, an email to Rich's family will be more than generous."

He persisted, with sparks of kindness in his voice.

"It will be no problem. I'll leave the store about 10:45 and should be at Rich and Julie's house by 2:30 a.m. I know the way very well. I used to live in Indiana. I'll call when I'm twenty minutes out."

As I descended the stairs to tell my story to the kids, I was overwhelmed with disbelief. And so were they. We decided to stay up and greet Dalton with the lights burning inside and outside in a welcoming fashion. Unaware of the miracle unfolding, Julie and Rich slept soundly. They would know nothing until the morning.

Quietly, each of us watched the family room clock tick away the hours, then minutes, then seconds. It was a sacred countdown. Waves of weariness were balanced with each exciting tick of the clock. Dalton was on the way, and getting closer. As promised, he called at 2:10 in the morning, to say he was twenty minutes away. It really was happening. Steve's Pizza was being delivered in the middle of the night, even though they don't offer delivery and were 220 miles away. Christopher and I went outside to watch for the flickering of car lights brightening up the starlit night. There he was, turning at the corner, and entering the driveway, as though it was a place he had been a thousand times. He stepped out of his car, two huge, flat boxes in hand and said,

"Here are your pizzas—pepperoni and mushroom."

Are there eighteen-year-old angels? Can they be five-foot-ten with reddish-blonde hair? Do they project love and caring in their voice and have a pleasant smile? If so, then we were in the presence of an angel—who drives a Honda. We hugged Dalton, thanking him profusely for his journey of mercy and invited him inside. All the grandkids reached out to him. We asked him to spend the night, to have something to drink or eat, to which he answered,

"Thanks, but I have to get back. I need to go to work in a few hours."

As he began to leave, he paused, turned around, and said,

"God bless you. I'm really sorry."

Christopher and I walked him to his car. I offered him money for the pizzas, gas and the seven hours of driving. He graciously refused. I took his hand and pressed the bills into his palm anyway. He left quietly into the night, from whence he had come. He had to be an angel.

Inside the house the two pizzas were placed secretly on the bottom shelf of the refrigerator. Morning was only a few hours away. Rich would awaken with his incessant cough, and Julie would stay close to comfort him. The rest of us would soon be at their bedside, celebrating the unexplainable events of a few hours ago. Three hours passed, and the sun introduced the new day. Rich had made it through another night.

We gathered by Rich's bedside; it felt like Christmas morning. There was a present that needed opening. Rich's daughter Elizabeth began to speak.

"Mommy and Daddy, do you like pizza?"

Rich feebly nodded, and Julie said profoundly,

"You know we do. We love pizza."

Elizabeth continued.

"Do you have a favorite pizza place?"

Uttering a reply with surprised amazement, Julie said,

"Sure...you ALL know how much we love Steve's Pizza."

Elizabeth went on to reveal the big secret.

"Well, Mommy and Daddy, we have two Steve's Pizzas in the refrigerator for you. They were delivered in the middle of the night."

Visible disbelief crept over their stunned faces. As the story unfolded, we all ate with overwhelming gratitude.

Our eyes needed to see, our ears needed to hear and our hearts needed to feel the presence of unconditional love. Indeed, it was a spirit-filled moment.

It was a parable.

WINTER

SNOOKY LANSON

In the middle of the 1950's, black-and-white television sets were a luxury for many American families. Certain programs during the decade were undoubtedly favorites and commanded the undivided attention of many avid viewers. One such broadcast was "Your Hit Parade", with Roy Landman, or his never-to-be-forgotten stage name, Snooky Lanson. Fortuitously he was invited to replace Frank Sinatra on this increasingly popular show.

Every Saturday at 7:00 p.m. I would sit with my family on a heavily-upholstered, gaudy davenport and watch "Your Hit Parade". With one television and very limited channels it was mind-boggling that we could, elbow to elbow, share in the anticipation and experience. Tonight's show was extra special. The music was the culmination of the Advent Season and the welcoming of Christmas Day. Each vocalist expressed the grandeur of this heavenly night. We sat captivated and motionless.

Everyone had sung except our favorite, Snooky Lanson. This was the finale. With divine poise he bowed his head. The orchestral accompaniment began. He slowly looked into the camera and with reverence began,

"O Holy Night, the stars are brightly shining."

In rapt attention we reached out for the words as he continued,

"It is the night of our dear Savior's birth. Long lay the...long lay...um...the..."

He forgot the words. Yes. He absolutely forgot the words! This was live television. He stumbled, continuing to look into the camera, as he hummed and fumbled for the elusive lyrics.

We squirmed and fidgeted, feeling his awkwardness. We wanted to jump through the television screen and shout the words to him: "Long lay the world in sin and error pining, 'til He appeared and the soul felt its worth." With apparent jitters, Snooky Lanson finally recalled his words and regrouped his composure. "Your Hit Parade" was the topic of conversation for the rest of the evening.

The next morning, the Sunday before Christmas, we went to church. We sang the joyful hymns, prayed the Advent prayers, listened to scriptures about the Holy Family in Bethlehem, and nestled in for the preached Word. Our Pastor fumbled for a second with his notes on the pulpit, and then with a gentle smile, he leaned into the microphone and said,

"Did anyone see "Your Hit Parade" last night?"

There was a jovial response of one accord.

He continued, "Wasn't that Snooky Lanson something..."

Once again, laughter filled the sanctuary.

"...Wasn't he wonderful?..."

I thought, *Wonderful? What did he mean?*

"...He sang about life last night. About how we can live our lives, especially at this time of new birth."

We sat in stillness and absolute silence. He continued.

"You see, my friends, when Snooky Lanson, with thousands of television onlookers fixated on their screens—

forgot, yes he forgot the words—he didn't quit. He pulled it all together. 'O Holy Night' has never had more meaning than it did for all of us last night!"

A newborn baby in a simple, rough-hewn stable, on this Holy Night, cries out to remind us that, even though you may stumble, you can pick yourself up and keep singing.

Thank you, Snooky Lanson.

"Let me tell you a story..."

THE SPIRITED ELEVEN

The dream of a little ten-year old lad, shooting hoops in his driveway, was to someday play on a college basketball team. Imagining himself both player and sports announcer, he narrates out loud his dribble...then he fakes to the left...and drives to the right...he stops—then launches the blemished leathery, round object into the air. The buzzer sounds as the ball swishes through the quiet net. He throws his arms upward and cheers loudly, all by himself, in his make-believe arena.

Each year this fantasy becomes a reality for former ten-year-old kids—now grown-up college athletes—culminating their basketball careers in a sixty-eight-team tournament called March Madness.

Do you remember the year 1976? It was the Bicentennial Year when the United States celebrated 200 years since declaring independence. It was also the year when one hundred little fourth grade boys stood on the floor of an old, beat-up Salvation Army gymnasium while overly-zealous coaches recruited their teams insisting,

"Come play for me, our team will be the best!"

I will never forget that year because I was one of those coaches—but I stayed seated in the bleachers and just observed the selection frenzy.

How did I get there? The back-story begins one year earlier when my son Mike was in the third grade. He played on a Biddy Basketball Team in the Wichita Salvation Army League. I had enrolled him because of one particular rule: every boy was to play at least two quarters—except that my son's coach did not abide by the rule. He had his favorites. Some boys entered the game for a token one or two minutes--some boys didn't play at all. I talked to the coach and reminded him of the league's rule. His response?

"I am the coach. This is how I do it."

The Salvation Army Recreation Director told me they would tolerate this coach for the remainder of the year, but would not invite him back.

As Mike and I left one of his Saturday morning games, he began to cry. I said,

"Mike, I'm sorry you lost."

He looked at me with tears rolling down his cheeks and said,

"Dad, I'm not crying because we lost. I'm crying because I didn't get to play."

And then came the biggest request of his young life:

"Next year, I want you to coach!"

That is how I found myself, one year later, sitting in the bleachers watching eager coaches select their teams. This selection process seemed unfair to the boys that were initially overlooked. I chose to stay there and not enter in. Finally, there were eleven boys left down on the hardwood. My son was one of them. The Recreation Director took a seat next to me and said,

"There's your team, only we have a problem. There are eleven boys and you can only pick ten."

I said, "You mean one of those boys will be left out?"

"Well, that is the rule," he reiterated.

With unwavering passion for fairness, I stated forcefully, "I won't do that. I take all eleven boys or none at all."

Later I told the team parents I had four coaching principles:

First—we will have fun and every boy will play in every game, at least two quarters.

Second—we will not worry about winning. The most points will not define the game for us.

Third—we will learn fundamentals like dribbling, passing and shooting.

As parents nodded their approval, I continued:

The Fourth principle is the most important—after each Saturday morning's game, I want to take our team out for some food.

The season wore on. There were no victories, but we were close a couple of times, with a few moments of excitement. Our center, Joey, was ecstatic as he ran by me on the bench and shouted,

"Coach, I scored!"

At the next time out, I told him it was a great shot—except it was in the wrong basket. And, I can't forget Scotty, of course. He was seated at the end of the bench, in the middle of a surprisingly close game, and shouted at me,

"Hey Coach, what are we having for lunch?"

Believe it or not, we were improving.

The last game was approaching. The team we were to play was undefeated and they took pleasure in reminding other teams of their winning record.

The day came, with three games scheduled that Saturday morning. We played in the first one. *I was certain we could not outscore them, but maybe we could out-scrap them.* Shockingly, when the first half ended, we were holding our own.

As the second half began, I noticed people streaming in for the next two games: parents, coaches, and young boys from other teams with their duffels strapped over their shoulders, waiting to play. The score of our game caught their attention. The crowd, now stirring with excitement, began cheering loudly for us. The seconds continued to count down. Soon the game was over. Except it wasn't actually over—we were tied! Overtime! The bright red numbers on the score clock urged on both teams—three more minutes. I looked at our sweaty little guys, breathing hard, and said to them,

"Just stay scrappy. You can beat this team. They are tired!"

Neither team scored for two minutes and fifty seconds.

Books are written and movies are made about the next ten seconds.

There was a jump ball under our basket. Before the restart, I called a time-out. In the nervous huddle I looked directly at Joey and said,

"You will be jumping. I want you to jump so high you hit your head on the ceiling of this gym. Tip the ball to Henry."

With the boys closely listening to my words, I continued,

"Henry, you like football, right?"

He replied, "I love football!"

I asked him—even though I knew the answer,

"What position do you play?"

With confidence and pride, he replied,

"I play quarterback."

With my eyes fixed on his, I said,

"Joey is going to tip the ball to you and I want you to act like a quarterback—catch the tip and spin around on your pivot foot so your back is to the basket."

I shifted my gaze to Mike.

"I want you to run to Henry and he will hand you the ball. Take the shot immediately. Am I clear?"

With our hands stacked together, I looked at each boy, knowing these next exciting moments could crown their season. Before we broke our huddle, I reassured them and said,

"You guys have ten seconds to pull off our *secret play*."

The referee threw the ball into the air. Joey nearly jumped out of the gymnasium and tipped it to Henry, who then pivoted like a seasoned quarterback, handing the ball off to a streaking Mike who launched it skyward. Time stood still as the ball took wings toward the open hoop. The buzzer sounded just as it swished through the waiting basket—we did it! We won!

As the years have moved along, tournaments and victory parades have made their way into the record books. But, I dare say, never will anything equal the excitement of those eleven little fourth-grade boys victoriously jumping up and down with disbelief, then with shouts of unbelievable joy and huge smiles on their young faces. Here they stood on an old Salvation Army gym floor, with parents, friends, players and coaches spilling from the bleachers to hug them—this same team who had scored in the wrong basket, and wondered amidst a close game,

"Hey Coach, what are we having for lunch?"

"Let me tell you a story..."

AN ANGELIC STAREDOWN

It was two days after Christmas and I made the annual trek to Kansas for a belated celebration. As grandparents we have learned the importance of allowing our grown children and their families to establish their own traditions. We would join them later. This was one of those times.

The evening was dwindling. Holiday shows were fading from the TV screen. One by one, family members peeled away from their warm, tucked-in places and trundled to their bedrooms. The living room—still blessed with historical, shiny ornaments and blinking lights—continued to wrap its arms around my youngest daughter and me. Three candles flickered heavenward. The two of us still remained, feeling nurtured by the silence of the moment. Appreciating the moment, I said,

"You and Pat have been the best parents to these grown kids. You need to hug yourselves."

She offered a humble response, and then there was more quietness.

Messages about the sacredness of life often occur in many forms. We don't program them. We don't anticipate them. Breaking the silence, I heard the softness of Mary Beth's voice:

"Dad, look at the wall—just to the right of the fireplace."

No more explanation was needed. There was an unmistakable image of an angel poised on the wall, in full color. We stared in amazement. Rising from our comfortable chairs we sidled up to stand next to each other in the middle of the living room. Would this angel be proclaiming to us like the shepherds watching over their flocks by night? *Do not be afraid—I bring you good news of great joy…*

Gerald Jampolsky, famed psychiatrist, said there are two basic emotions—love and fear. We were experiencing both of them. There were no angel decorations in the room to cast a reflection. We kept turning lights on and off, and yet the image remained, almost taunting us to accept the announcement from on high—the eternal promise.

We became aware of a snow globe on a table near the Christmas tree. In it was a holiday scene, with snow falling. Looking at the globe, we noticed a slight crack in the glass. It created a prism that separated the white light into a spectrum of wondrous colors. Out of this came our angelic image—a perfect, unannounced angel—radiantly displayed on the wall, staring at us. We stared back. The message was clear: *Do not be afraid…I bring you good news.*

"Let me tell you a story..."

AN UNMISTAKABLE GIFT

It is an age-old question: *How does God speak to us?* Answers abound—the beckoning of a wind-blown leaf—the blinking of a street light—a gentle snowflake alighting on the end of your cold nose—the first smile of a newborn baby—the sun glistening off a mountain peak—or the voice of a friend.

I have often thought that God speaks to us most profoundly through others. Sometimes, it is the eloquence of words on a printed page that leaps out at us. They grab our attention and won't let go. We may carry their meaning with us throughout the entire day, dawn to dusk. We might even consider behaving differently. I don't remember the author or the book's title, but these words from the heart of an old sage are still my mantra: "Give as much of yourself as you can to as much of every situation as you understand."

Then, there is Bruce. We have been confidantes and trustworthy friends for decades. We have not allowed one another to dangle helplessly during our moments of despair or emotional wounding. I dialed his phone.

"It's David. I need some guidance."

Within three hours, we were gazing earnestly at each other, coffee cups in hand, elbows leaning on our scarred, old kitchen table. He was curious and very present. I was disorganized with my thoughts—it didn't matter. I began to ramble about a decision I needed to make. I was stuck and nothing was clear. *O God, show me a sign. Nudge me one way or another.*

I wanted Bruce to tell me what to do. But good friends don't do for us what we need to do for ourselves. Answers are often tucked inside us, just waiting to be discovered and expressed. We took a short, brisk walk on that wintry day. Often, perplexed minds and wondering hearts begin to take on new clarity when we are in motion. As we walked, I kept waiting for a bright light of direction to shine on me. We returned.

My head was bowed in contemplation when Bruce wisely asked,

"Well, David, how much time do you have?"

"Oh, I have the rest of the afternoon."

Slightly scolding, he said,

"That's not what I meant and I believe you know that."

He asked again, "How much time do you have?"

I tipped my head back, pondering as I looked at the empty ceiling.

"I'm not sure what you mean."

Once again, he asked,

"How much time do you have?"

I felt like a floundering fish being pulled from its damp haven; he would not let me off the hook. Then—like a bolt of wisdom from the heavens—I realized the intent of his question: *How much time do you have—to do the things that are important to you?*

God had spoken through the human voice of a friend—an unmistakable gift.

"Let me tell you a story..."

THE UTTERMOST TEST

Wisdom grows out of our experiences. As the multi-talented entertainer, Danny Kaye, said,

"Life is a great big canvas, and you should throw all the paint you can on it."

With each thought, feeling and behavior we grow wiser. Life-changing decisions deserve meditation and contemplation. However, it is the everyday choices that ultimately test us. It is the spontaneously unplanned events that expose our deepest values, that cause us to wonder: *What is the most loving response I can make in this unexpected situation?*

I have not always had emotionally satisfying experiences with airplane flights. I have missed connections, not arrived on time and been bumped. Today, as I boarded the winged giant, I longed for a pleasant, uncomplicated trip. The de-icing was finished and we were airborne.

As we greeted the fluffy clouds at 35,000 feet in the air, flight attendants delivered our drinks. I chose tomato juice and set the unopened miniature can on my tray. It was time for a short nap before indulging myself. An hour passed. I awoke only to notice all the drinks had been picked up, except mine, and everyone around me was soundly asleep, especially the gentleman across the aisle from me. He was obviously relaxing for a big meeting. He had on a crisp white dress shirt, striped tie and meticulously creased slacks.

It was time for my deferred treat. Being a tomato juice connoisseur, I shook the can vigorously and snapped open the metal latch. Red juice dramatically sprayed like an Old Faithful eruption, sending droplets spewing across the aisle, landing softly on his pristine shirt. He slept, unaware. I drank my juice and quickly disposed of the can. The bright spots began to fade into a subtle, dull pink, but still noticeable. Everyone around me was still sleeping. *How is he going to know it was me? I mean, the spots just might fade totally out by the time he opens his eyes.* Rationalization set in: *This is not a Bill of Rights issue and isn't a serious health care decision or setting up water purifiers in Kenya.*

I remembered the story the ancient Greek philosopher Socrates told about a magic ring. Whoever wore it would become invisible, and thus avoid any consequences for his or her actions. I wanted to put that ring on my finger. The landing announcement from the flight attendant jarred everyone from their slumber. He woke up. Out of the corner of my eye I saw him touching his polka-dotted shirt. I heard a low guttural sound as he was shaking his head from side to side. I continued my steadfast forward gaze. While descending agonizingly slowly to the runway. I made a decision. *I had to confess.* I leaned his way and told him the whole story. With deep apology I offered to give him some money to purchase a new shirt.

Socrates' ring reminds us we are tested every day. We do not live in isolation. We live in communities and in relationships. It is a big canvas that we splatter with paint from life's decisions. Let us never forget: our values and ethics are involved in everything we say and do, and everything we say and do matters.

SOMEONE'S MESSIN' WITH THE LIGHTS

During my first year out of graduate school I was appointed to serve on the staff of a large church in the middle of wheat country. Bill, my mentor, and the Senior Minister of the church, was an affable, soft-spoken gentleman with an ample amount of pastoral savvy. My life thrived with him at my side.

One Fall afternoon, Bill asked me to take a walk with him. He was grim-faced and spoke with a somber voice.

"David, Carl Michalson was killed in an airplane crash yesterday. He was going to Cincinnati to speak at a Christian Education conference. I'm so sorry. I know how much you respected him as your teacher."

My heart left my body. No professor was more crucial in my theological search for my place in this world.

I understand that sometime before, Carl's brother, the Reverend Gordon Michalson, had told a story about a pact the brothers made with one another regarding death. Whoever died first was to send an unmistakable sign to the other validating that all of what they had been teaching was real. The message? *There is a God. God loves us. There is life after death.*

The day after Carl's tragic accident, New York City had a blackout. Was this the brotherly sign? Or—should it just be chalked up to coincidence? Gordon was heard to say: *I can just picture Carl playing around with the cosmic switchboard!* My curiosity was piqued; someone was messin' with the lights.

Several years later, after I moved to Colorado, my dad died. Christmas was approaching. Our family tradition loomed, this time shrouded with gloom and melancholy. Historically, our Christmas celebrations, usually held in Kansas, were synonymous with indescribable elation and lightheartedness—except for this year. Everyone came to our home in Colorado. It was also a year of severe storms.

The heavy snow drove a feeling of angst into everyone's flying or driving. However, rugged determination to still be celebrative—even in Dad's absence—was the impetus that brought us together. Everyone had arrived and was asleep. I laid on the couch, grateful that all were safe. I softly hummed "Silent Night" as I stared at the ceiling fan, transfixed by its rhythm. Then it happened—like a bolt from the snowy sky— the ceiling light near the front door flashed on!

The bulb had not shone for years. Electricians had told us the wiring was faulty. I moved in slow motion towards the foyer light. I flicked the switch up and down several times, and yet the filaments continued to shine, glowing brighter than ever before. Reverently, I looked upward,

"Is that you, Dad?"

Not sure what possessed me to wing those words heavenward. *I suppose if Dr. Michalson could mess with the cosmic switchboard and cause a blackout in all of New York City, Dad could surely unleash his spirit on this little home.* I retreated to the couch. There, I laid awake for several hours rehearsing what I would tell the family. The light went off.

The sun rose, creating sparkles to dance on the fresh snow. Everyone was jovial, casually mentioning how much fun Dad would be having if he were with us. I decided to reveal what had happened only a few hours ago. I wasn't sure if their rapt attention meant they believed me, or if they were just being courteous. I even flipped the light switch to demonstrate how unworkable it was. With a shrug of my shoulders, I suggested that perhaps Dad's spirit is hovering—somehow.

It was evening and time for our traditional Christmas Eve meal. We acknowledged Dad's absence and gave ourselves permission to feel the tears, as we stood and prayed our blessing. It was time to light the candle on the fireplace mantle located by the foyer. As I pressed the lighted match to the wick, I playfully sang,

"And the angel Gabriel lit the candle..." and the light abruptly came on—as if on cue. Awestruck, we all stared. My oldest daughter, Julie, said,

"It's Grandpa."

My son Mike just looked amazed and uttered,

"No way."

Mary Beth, my youngest, could only whisper,

"This is weird."

Mom didn't say a word.

The light remained on while we shared one of Dad's favorite meals. All of a sudden, the entranceway became dark. We noticed, looked at each other, and continued chatting and laughing with underlying sadness. After the meal, Mom tearfully suggested we all gather around the piano and sing some carols. It was her loving effort to put her arms around all of us—much like Dad had done for many years. She sat down at the keyboard. We sang the old favorites. Eventually she said,

"Let's see if we can sing 'Silent Night'—it was always Dad's favorite," tenderly calling him Dad at that moment. Then, as she played the first chord on the piano, the light in the foyer went on! Truth had spoken. He was with us—in spirit.

As the days passed, lights blinked off and on throughout the house and on street lamps. I believe it was Dad's way of saying to all of us:

Do not be afraid.

Maybe, just maybe, he was messin' with the lights.

"Let me tell you a story..."

HIS NAME IS KNUCKLEHEAD

Picture with me a snowy, blustery Christmas Eve. The carolers have gone to their homes. Scrumptious meals send aromas wafting out chimneys. Shouts of joy for happily-met hopes pour from the voices of children while opening their presents. For some, their dreams have been answered. Church bells cut through the darkness, welcoming worshippers to the services.

The Animal Hospital on Main Street, adorned with brightly colored lights, is finally closing. It has been a long day for the weary and dedicated staff. Gathering up leftover sugar cookies from today's party, many exit the back door. "Merry Christmas!" "You, too!"

Jennifer, a staff assistant, thinking she is the last to leave, moves toward the front door to latch it, just as it slowly opens. Standing in the swirling snow is a bedraggled young man, holding a puppy shivering against his greasy, grimy coat. With a quivering voice, he utters,

"I hope you can help me. My dog is so sick."

Jennifer opens the door wider.

"Come in."

She takes her coat off, and moves purposefully behind a desk.

"What is your dog's name?"

"His name is, um, his name is Knucklehead."

"And, what is your name?"

"My name is Lonnie. I work at the junkyard outside of town. Knucklehead keeps me company. I sure hope you can help him."

Quiet desperation fills the empty room that had been so alive not long ago with yelping sounds and dangling leashes.

Jennifer took Knucklehead from Lonnie's loving grasp and went into the examination room. To her surprise one of the doctors was still finishing his paperwork. Together they began an impromptu examination of their limp, sickly companion. Lonnie waited, hungry, tired, and alone. He stared at the floor, prayerfully. Church bells continued to accompany his reverie.

Twenty minutes later Jennifer took a seat next to Lonnie. She softly said,

"We believe Knucklehead has parvovirus, a disease of the intestines. I invite you not to worry—we'll take good care of him. We'll give him lots of fluids and also antibiotics. He needs to stay with us for at least a week."

Lonnie rubbed his forehead. He could not look up. He mumbled,

"I don't have much money, and..."

Jennifer interrupted,

"Don't worry about the money. We will talk about that later. Please come back in one week. You can also call me to see how Knucklehead is doing. Here's my card with my name and telephone number on it."

During that week Lonnie pawned his old pickup truck to pay for the Animal Hospital bill. One week, to the day,

Lonnie returned. The Christmas lights surrounding the doorframe were still blinking.

"Knucklehead is much better," said Jennifer. "Here are some medications with instructions on how you must give them to him."

Lonnie fumbled in his old, shaggy jeans pocket for the money from the sale of his pickup. Jennifer placed her hand on his and said once again,

"We can talk about money later."

Lonnie was so overwhelmed with gratitude, and with a belief that Christmastime is full of miracles, he went to the local newspaper and told them his story: how he had gone to the Animal Hospital unannounced, five minutes before closing on Christmas Eve, and how they had cured his puppy. He cried when he told them. The newspaper printed his story with a picture of Lonnie and Knucklehead on the front page.

Folks began calling the Animal Hospital and the newspaper to donate clothing and money for Lonnie, and give praise to the clinic. One man read about the story on an animal website. A five-year-old girl with a gentle spirit came by the Hospital to give three dollars for Knucklehead's bill. It was money she had received for Christmas. Another man searched endlessly to find Lonnie's pawned pickup truck, and repurchased it for him. Two exciting days later, Jennifer called Lonnie.

"You had better come to the hospital. We have lots of stuff for you!"

Upon arriving at the Hospital, he was led to a back room full of blankets, clothes and an ample amount of money. Jennifer looked compassionately at Lonnie.

"All this is yours. It is for you."

Silence filled the room. Lonnie could barely find words or sound.

"Well, I could use a blanket or two, and...I guess...some clothes. I want you to keep the money and give it to someone who can't pay their bill."

Each Christmas I picture Lonnie kneeling at the stable, holding a healthy puppy close to his grimy coat, grateful for another miracle.

HEY...JESUS IS OVER HERE

Have you ever been in a live Nativity scene? It is a sacred, seasonal pageant that usually begins two weeks before Christmas Day and ends on Christmas Eve. Folks of all ages become characters of yesteryear, dressing up in costumes reminiscent of Biblical times. Animals mill about the grassy grounds near the makeshift stable while music plays over loudspeakers. The pageant takes on life—as we imagine it was. Onlookers stop on the sidewalk to observe, while carloads of families drive by night after night to park and listen.

During my senior year of college, I decided to be a Wiseman in my home church's live Nativity. It was an undertaking of mammoth proportions—fourteen straight nights with three presentations each evening—it challenged my commitment. My devotion to the Biblical message didn't deter my mildly-suppressed inner excitement for the nights to hurry by. I was the last Wiseman to enter the scene, exiting the side door of our large church building. I carried the Frankincense. To add drama, I would put a piece of dry ice in a basin of water, and it would steam into the night. My character was inspiring. Each night, I would wind my way through the animals, shepherds and townsfolk before kneeling at the manger, and offering my gift.

It was Christmas Eve. The pageant was drawing to a close. Last minute onlookers crowded the street in front of the church as we prepared for our last rendering. The sounds of "We Three Kings" rang into the night. We lined up just inside the church for our final entrance onto the lawn and to the waiting baby in the manger. One of the Wisemen noticed that my basin of water had a very small piece of dry ice in it, while there were several pieces left over.

"Why waste them?" he declared, throwing all of them into the water. The door opened and I walked into the night, with new energy and a huge reaction of billowing steam coming from my bowl of water. The haze and fog were so thick that it blocked my vision and I became disoriented in my quest for the stable. I roamed aimlessly—bumping into angels, shepherds and animals. I was lost.

And then, cutting through the tender sounds of the Wisemen's hymn, I heard a loud whisper,

"Hey...Jesus is over here."

With confidence and peace, I found my way.

THE OLD MAN IN THE SAUNA

Life's truisms can stop us in our tracks like a gust of wind blowing from the majestic mountains or dusty plains. They come to us on a slow jog on a country road or during a meditative walk in the neighborhood. These proverbs crawl inside our minds, hearts and deep in our souls. We have not invited them inside ourselves. They happen when we least expect them. They guide our steps from that moment on—especially on this blustery, snowy day.

My ritual at our local athletic club, before engaging in a racquetball match, was to sit in the sauna and finish dressing. The hissing steam embraced and relaxed my body. This particular day I noticed an older man in the sauna, sitting against the wall, towel draped over him. Seated alone, he was barely visible in the fogginess of the small cedar-walled room. I greeted him casually.

The silence was broken with the sound of a gravelly voice.

"Ya know, if I'd have known I was going to live this long, I'd have taken better care of myself."

Fumbling for a response, I simply said,

"Yes, I'm sure that is true."

I actually had heard those words before from older family members seeking to be humorous. More silence. He shifted his rickety, old body, and then said,

"You know you are getting old when you fall down and then try to figure out how many things you can do while you are down there."

I snickered, tipping my head back, as if to affirm the jocularity in his words. Somehow I suspected more was forthcoming from this old man in the sauna. I was right.

"You know, young man, I quit drinkin' a few years ago. Guess I'll live longer. I s'pose that's a good deal."

Something inside of me wanted to reach out to this sweaty soul. But it was time for me to go play. I said,

"Well...guess I better leave you for now. Maybe I'll see you again. Take good care of yourself."

Dressing for the match, I pulled my shirt down over my moist torso and started to push the door open. I was playing that day in one of my favorite shirts, given to me by my son-in-law, a firefighter in Lawrence, Kansas. On the back it read,

COMMITTED TO SAVING LIVES

As I opened the door the old man, with the wisdom of Solomon, said in an elevated and expressive voice,

"Committed to savin' lives, huh? Well, someone has got to save us from ourselves."

Indeed, a truism, when I least expected it...

CPSIA information can be obtained
at www.ICGtesting.com
Printed in the USA
FSHW021805260821
84026FS